(front cover)   Wooden models found at Roos Carr near Hull – possibly representing a Bronze Age logboat and crew.

(back cover)   Photographic montage of the excavated impression of Sutton Hoo boat 2 in 1939.
Photo: Miss M. Lack.

ACKNOWLEDGEMENT

I wish to thank John Coates, Professor John Evans, Dr Basil Greenhill, Professor Adrian Horridge, Keith Muckelroy, Dr Derek Roe and Dr Piet van der Merwe who critically read sections from an early draft. I am responsible for any errors in the published text.

Seán McGrail

In Memory of Keith Muckelroy

ISBN 0 11 290312 6

Design by HMSO Graphic Design

Printed in England for
Her Majesty's Stationery Office
by Balding & Mansell, Wisbech, Cambs

Dd 696325   C160

National Maritime Museum

THE SHIP

Rafts, Boats and Ships

From Prehistoric Times to the Medieval Era

Sean McGrail

London
Her Majesty's Stationery Office

Contents

Plate 1   Building a 20th century Peruvian reed raft. Drawing after Edwards, 1965, plate 1.

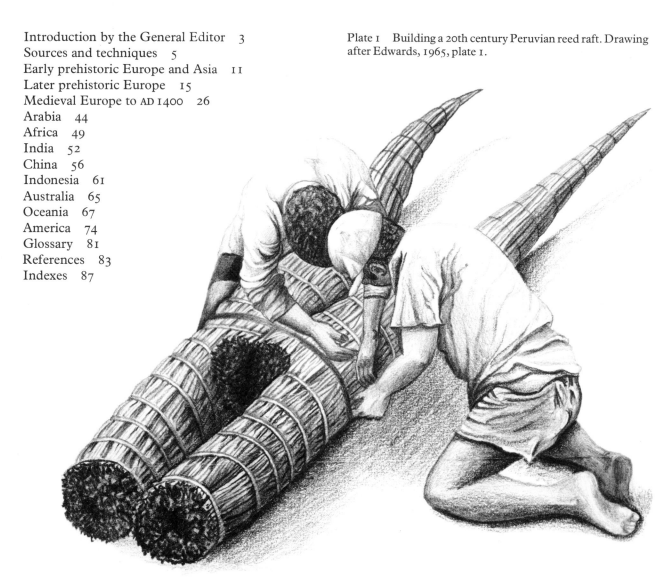

Introduction by the General Editor

This is the first of a series of ten short books on the development of the ship, both the merchant vessel and the specialised vessel of war, from the earliest times to the present day, commissioned and produced jointly by The National Maritime Museum and Her Majesty's Stationery Office. The books are each self-contained, each dealing with one aspect of the subject, but they cover the evolution of vessels in terms which are detailed, accurate and up-to-date. They incorporate the latest available information and the latest thinking on the subject, but they are readily intelligible to the non-specialist, professional historian or layman.

Above all, as should be expected from the only large and comprehensive general historical museum in the world which deals especially with the impact of the sea on the development of human culture and civilisation, the approach is unromantic and realistic. Merchant ships were, and are, machines for carrying cargo profitably. They carried the trade and, in the words of the very distinguished author of the second book in this series, 'The creation of wealth through trade is at the root of political and military power'. The vessel of war, the maritime vehicle of that power, follows and she is a machine for men to fight from, or with.

It follows from such an approach that the illustrations to the series are for the most part from contemporary sources. The reader can form his own conclusions from the evidence, written and visual.

In this, the first book of the series, Dr Seán McGrail deals with the development of ships generally all over the world from prehistoric to medieval times. He does so in a masterly, comprehensive study, of a kind which has not been published before, drawing together the evidence from multiple sources, archaeological, iconographic, ethnographic and literary. He emphasizes that the study of the archaeology of water transport still stands on the threshold of its development. It is very much in the descriptive, data-collecting, stage and only after evidence has been carefully recorded and assessed can we proceed to the analytical stage and the development of hypotheses. In only a few very limited fields has the study and recording proceeded so far that building traditions can begin to be identified – as perhaps they can with the Viking ships of Dark Age Europe and the cogs of the medieval Hanseatic community.

Nevertheless, by the adoption of a systematic structure, Dr McGrail carries the reader through this highly complex mass of information in a manner which gives it form and cohesion and which makes reference to individual sections easy. This book will be immensely useful to those involved in any way with the archaeology of water transport. It sets new standards as a general background picture and as a work of reference.

Dr McGrail, Chief Archaeologist at The National Maritime Museum, is also the Head of the Museum's Archaeological Research Centre. He and his staff are the only group of their kind in the world dedicated to the full-time professional study of the development of boats and ships until the fifteenth century.

Basil Greenhill
DIRECTOR, NATIONAL MARITIME MUSEUM
General Editor

3

Plate 2

Plate 3

Plate 4

Plate 2   Early 19th century Tasmanian bark bundle rafts from Lesueur and Petit's *Terre de Diémen*.

Plate 3   A 20th century buoyed raft on the River Swat, northern Pakistan. Photo: Ann Bamford.

Plate 4   19th century drawing of a sailing log raft from Gambier Is., Tuamotu Archipelago, Polynesia.

Plate 5   A modern *zaima* reed boat of the southern Iraq marshes made of reed bundles with an inserted light framework and waterproofed with bitumen. Photo: plate 45 in *Marsh Arabs* by Wilfred Thesiger.

Plate 5

Sources and techniques

General considerations

The importance of water transport   Basil Greenhill (1976, 27) has described the boats of the Vikings and the Polynesians as not only their supreme technical achievement but also their principal aesthetic and social feat. Water transport at other times and places may not have been so singularly superlative, but of its importance to Man throughout the period covered by this book there can be no doubt. From at least Upper Palaeolithic times, *c* 40 000 years ago, water-borne craft have been essential for the exploitation of lake, river and sea, the colonisation of new lands and the sustainment of trade.

Basic types of water transport   It is convenient to classify water transport by the raw material principally used in construction: wood, reed, bark, hide and so on (although other characteristics such as the sequence and techniques of building are important when defining individual traditions). These may then be divided into three groups: *personal aids* to flotation with the man partly immersed in the water; *rafts*, which are not watertight but obtain their buoyancy from the qualities of individual elements; and *boats* with a (near) watertight hull deriving buoyancy from displacement of water. Certain rafts may be 'boat-shaped', but as they are not watertight they are not boats. Conversely, a coracle, although of round form, is a boat.

Using these criteria nine basic types of raft and boat may be identified:

RAFTS

1 Reed raft: bound bundles of reed, lashed together (Plate 1) (rafts of light timbers bound in bundles may also be included e.g. *ambatch* rafts of the White Nile).

2 Bark raft: bound bark bundles lashed together (Plate 2).

3 Buoyed raft: a lashed wooden framework given extra buoyancy by skin floats, gourds or sealed pots etc. (Plate 3).

4 Log raft: logs or bamboos lashed together, with varying degrees of elaboration (Plate 4).

BOATS

5 Reed boat: bound bundles of reed lashed together (coiled basketry) to produce a hollow form and waterproofed with bitumen (Plate 5).

6 Bark boat: a sheet of bark or several sheets sewn together, sometimes with an internal wooden structure (Plate 6).

7 Skin boat: a framework of woven basketry or an open wooden framework, covered by waterproof material such as hide, canvas, bitumen, dung etc. (Plate 7) (a hide alone may be used).

8 Logboat: a hollowed log (Plate 8) ('dugout canoe'); some may be expanded or may have members added. Complex ones are better classified as planked boats.

9 Planked boat: wooden planks and other elements joined by sewing, or by wooden or metal fastenings. This has proved to be the most flexible and adaptable, resulting in innumerable variants differentiated by function, form, size, boatbuilding techniques and means of propulsion.

This classification may not be ideal – for example the 'buoyed raft' may be thought of as a hybrid; rafts of light timbers bound in bundles might form a separate group; and craft such as the tub-boats described by Hornell (1970, fig. 11), cannot easily be included. Nevertheless, it defines terms and can form a basis for discussion.

Invention, diffusion, evolution   Arguments have sometimes been advanced for the diffusion of particular forms of water transport from an assumed place of origin. Paul Johnstone (1980, 40) for example, considers the skin boat may have been devised during Upper Palaeolithic times in the central Eurasian landmass between the River Don and River Dnieper, and the concept diffused down rivers to the coasts. A boat is indeed 'her own advertisement' and a successful design, or aspects of it, may be easily diffused. Detailed research to establish such diffusion has seldom been undertaken, however, and an opposing view that similar requirements and similar resources may have resulted in the invention of some of the basic types of water transport independently in different times and places should also be considered.

Again, it is sometimes said that certain craft, widely separated in time and space, are alike. For example, 20th century Portuguese boats are said to resemble those of ancient Mesopotamia. Such similarities are almost invariably not in building techniques but in form, which may be explained without recourse to diffusionist theory. Certain shapes are more suitable than others for a particular operating environment or function. Thus, other things being equal, a rectangular transverse section carries more payload than a rounded one, but has more resistance to motion; and overhanging bows are useful for a river ferry but impracticable in a sea boat. Today we find similarly shaped boats carrying out similar functions in comparable environments, but widely separated in space. It thus seems possible that in former times, in separate but similar regions (environmentally and technologically), similar *forms* of boat were evolved. Where different building techniques were used – different sequences of assembling the elements, different ways of lashing the reed bundles, different methods of caulking and so on – it is not necessary to postulate contact or even indirect influence. On the other hand, similarities in building techniques or in handling methods are probably more indicative of diffusion of ideas or migration.

The possible evolution of planked boats from other forms of water transport is also much argued. As this generates more heat than light the question is best left open until more data are available.

The evidence

Excavated evidence   Watercraft are made from perishable materials and thus the surviving remains of early Man may give the impression that he was land bound. Nevertheless in favourable circumstances, bark, wood and other organic materials used in boatbuilding do survive to be excavated, albeit with a strong bias towards logboats and planked craft. But recovery and examination do not guarantee understanding and interpretation. Especially is this true when – as is most often the case – only fragments are recovered. Nor does understanding guarantee that this achievement will be presented to a wider audience: and only by publication – in book, lecture or display – can the results be critically evaluated and their relationships to other problems established, with the resulting general advance in knowledge. It will be seen, therefore, that data may be lost at all stages between the moment of deposition and the present day. Archaeologists aim to minimise this loss of information and to compensate for it by reasoned argument.

One of the most difficult problems is that of dating. There are three ways of attempting to date excavated craft:

by consideration of the craft's form and structure;

by dating the context of the find; and

by dating the materials used to build the craft.

However, the special nature of boat finds means that only rarely can all these potential methods be used (McGrail, 1978, 8) and the third method of dating, by radiocarbon assay or by dendrochronological analysis is often the only practical one. Such work has only recently been undertaken and thus relatively few reliable dates are available.

Iconographic evidence   Iconographic evidence may sometimes be the only evidence available: sails and rigging rarely survive to be excavated, but stone carvings, engravings on seals or pottery decorations may depict these fittings and their method of use. On the other hand, iconography can be unrepresentative of the contemporary range of water transport in use: medieval seals almost invariably feature ships rather than rafts or boats.

 This sort of evidence is relatively plentiful in the medieval period, but it is varied in quality and difficult to interpret (Farrell, 1979; McGrail and Farrell, 1979). Prehistoric evidence being generally more stylistic can be even more difficult to understand. However, analysis of individual decorative elements and comparisons between representations from the same culture may allow working hypotheses to be formulated about artistic conventions: for example, vertical lines on the hull may represent bindings for a reed raft; vertical lines above the hull may represent men; horizontal lines along the hull may represent planking; and a craft with low length/freeboard ratio may represent a skin boat riding high in the water. But these are guidelines not rules, and it may be necessary to admit that some representations cannot

be fully interpreted. Compounding these difficulties is the problem of ascribing a date and an origin to the depicted boat: without these the material can be of little use to nautical archaeology. Art historical criteria are sometimes used uncritically to suggest a date, and the margin of error involved may be insufficiently stressed.

Documentary evidence   Written evidence may include an account by a 16th century traveller, an Icelandic saga, an early coastal pilot, or a Sumerian clay tablet. Recording the building or the use of a boat is seldom the main purpose of such records thus the nautical information may frequently be inconsequential. Additionally, there are problems in assessing the reliability and the nautical competence of the observer, and in giving the document a precise provenance in time and space. Translators with inadequate knowledge of boats may compound these problems, as may the fact that no modern English word may exist to describe certain features or operations. If these difficulties can be overcome and the documents critically assessed, they can not only fill gaps in the history of water transport but also provide comparative evidence useful when interpreting fragmentary excavated material.

Ethnographic evidence   Accounts of simple forms of water transport still, or recently, in use are of value in compiling regional histories of water transport, providing cultural continuity can be established. They may also be used cross-culturally to provide a range of possibilities for the archaeologist to consider when attempting to interpret excavated material. The likelihood of a valid parallel being drawn will be increased the more similar the two cultures can be shown to be.

 Some ethnographic accounts emphasise the spectacular at the expense of the general, and contain an indifferent record of boatbuilding and mode of use.

Diagrams could clarify and amplify such records, but these are infrequent. Exceptionally, Hornell in *Water Transport* (1970) and in other publications provides an incomparable range of material, which can be supplemented by detailed studies such as that by Best (1925) of the Maori canoe, whilst recent work by Greenhill (1971) in the Indian sub-continent, and by McKee in Britain shows what can be achieved by thorough fieldwork.

The evidence worldwide　Not until the medieval period in parts of Europe and comparable stages in other regions do we have a range of evidence from the sources discussed above, and this is mainly about the principal types of planked ship and boat; evidence for craft made of other material is meagre. Not

until many more finds from the European medieval period are recorded can we be certain that we have an understanding of the full range of watercraft in use. In the prehistoric periods, even in the most favoured regions, evidence is discontinuous in time and space so that rather than a continuous history of water transport we get glimpses at a few locations.

In America, Oceania and Australia, there are few indigenous records before first contact by post-medieval European man, and excavation and the critical study of other evidence has only begun to reveal nautical information in the past few years. The best that can be done therefore is to establish details of the water transport in use at this first contact, before any European influence. With caution, similar work can be attempted for Arabia, Africa, India,

Plate 6　19th century drawing by Friedrich Ratzel of bark boats of Tierra del Fuego.

Plate 7　A simple form of skin boat (bull boat) used recently by Sioux Indians. Photo: Museum of the American Indian, New York.

Indonesia and China, despite contacts between these areas and intermittently with Europe from early times. Some of those contacts have in fact provided us with written evidence of water transport in non-literate areas, Classical authors being especially useful.

Techniques

Investigating a boat find Recording a find *in situ*, and again after excavation enables measured drawings and descriptions to be compiled. Evidence for missing fittings may be revealed and the sequence of the early stages of building probably becomes clear. Toolmarks, signs of wear and methods of repair are also invaluable evidence. As the individual elements are examined and related to one another a picture should begin to emerge, in so far as the evidence survives, of the vessel's internal support system, how the main elements are held together, the means of making her watertight (if a boat) and the propulsion and steering systems. Incomplete and unusual features may be better understood by reference to other contemporary finds, written descriptions, iconographic representations, or ethnographic parallels where this is justified.

The raw materials need to be identified and their relationship to their parent body determined. The criteria used by the ancient boatbuilder when selecting material and the method used to prepare it for use may then become clear: these factors may be of importance when attempting to recognise specific traditions.

Drawing on a knowledge of other contemporary finds, of seamanship and of naval architectural principles, a conjectural reconstruction may then be attempted, so that deductions may be made about use and performance. In general there will not be a unique solution to the problem of determining the original full shape of a fragmentary find, and several versions may be equally plausible, although the minimum solution is generally to be preferred. Associated material may help to determine how the craft was used. The site type – estuary, river, lake etc. – may also afford clues, although findspot is not necessarily where the craft was normally used. Form may also reflect function, as may certain fittings. If a full reconstruction drawing can be made hydrostatic curves may be drawn and from them displacement/ draft relationships established. Estimates may then be made of what the boat could have carried and how she could have behaved afloat. Small models may also be made and tested in an experimental tank to assess such qualities as speed. Finally the building and trials of a replica can give valuable insight into problems and solutions, and shed light on operational performance: for example, how close to the wind the original craft might have sailed (McGrail, 1977).

Classification Any attempt to comprehend a large body of data and recognise patterns requires abstraction and classification so that significant similarities and differences may be highlighted and a picture of general groupings emerge. Ideally, each boat find, representation or description should be recorded against a standard list of features. For example, a logboat may be described by 120 attributes grouped under headings: Date; Region; Function; Form; Propulsion; Speed potential; Size; Boatbuilding characteristics (McGrail and Switsur, 1979).

Analysis of this data may reveal regional or temporal groups with characteristic attributes. Diagnostic attributes, a subset of the latter, should then enable future finds, descriptions or representations to be allocated to one of these groups.

A group may prove to have attributes similar to those of well-documented, named types, e.g. cog or junk. This family name may then, with caution, be applied to the archaeologically identified group. Clear definition of attributes and groups is an essential prerequisite to this. Objects and concepts may have different names at different times and place, or the same term may be applied to dissimilar objects. The change in the meaning of the word 'hulc' from 15th century to the present day illustrates the latter point.

Application   In the remaining chapters of this book, all available forms of evidence are considered, region by region, to produce an account of the rafts, boats and ships used. The patchiness of this evidence and the incompleteness, or even absence, of research is reflected in the depth of treatment in individual chapters. It proved impossible to examine all the evidence at first hand and thus I have often had to use published material, some of which raised more questions than it answered.

In general, the study of early water transport is at the descriptive, data collection stage. Only after phenomena have been carefully observed and recorded can we proceed to the analytical phase. There are exceptions, however, where, in limited fields, recording has proceeded sufficiently far for boat-building traditions to be tentatively identified (e.g. Viking ships—see Crumlin-Pedersen, 1978; R. Mersey logboats—see McGrail and Switsur, 1979). On the other hand, in certain regions it is only possible to give an idea of the watercraft in use at first European contact.

Plate 8   The oak logboat excavated at Brigg, Lincolnshire, in 1886. Photo: Lincolnshire Library Services.

Early prehistoric Europe and Asia

The period discussed in this chapter is traditionally divided into five broad phases from the Lower Palaeolithic to the Neolithic, which are related to Man's technological progress and can be approximately equated with consecutive chronological periods, though at any one time different regions could be at different technological stages. In addition early forms of tools continued in use in later phases, and, as these phases each lasted for millennia, tools and techniques used at the end of a phase were not necessarily those in use at the beginning. Nevertheless, the concept of successive technological stages provides a useful framework for the discussion of boatbuilding.

Wooden artifacts, thought to be paddles, have been found on early sites suggesting the use of water transport but, apart from some hollowed logs of Mesolithic and Neolithic date, there are no remains of floats, rafts or boats from this era. Something may be learned, however, by charting in general terms Man's technological progress, his expanding tool kit, his use of raw materials and his mastery of specific techniques; this has been attempted in the first four columns of Table 1. Organic materials used by early Man survive only rarely and their use has often to be deduced indirectly: future finds may necessitate revision of the dates for earliest use given in the table.

If we then consider the simplest forms of float, raft and boat ever known to have been used by Man, we may tentatively deduce by analogy the earliest technological stage at which these basic types of water transport could have been built. These theo-

retical deductions are also listed in Table 1. Whether these types were indeed used at a particular time and place depends on the local availability of raw materials, and whether the idea of applying these tools and techniques to water transport had arisen.

Lower Palaeolithic (before 700 000 BC to *c* 200 000 BC)
During the milder climatic phases of this period, which approximately correspond with the Middle Pleistocene, *Homo erectus*, an ancestral species of Man probably originating in the central part of the African continent, came to inhabit a zone which included North Africa, western and central Europe and stretched as far east as Java and Peking. During times of lower sea level, these areas could have been reached by overland routes. However, many of the known settlements are on the margins of lakes or in river valleys (Clark, 1977, 31), and exploration, hunting and the gathering of food and raw materials could have been more effectively undertaken by the use of some form of water transport. In addition, it is likely that, some 500 000 to 300 000 years ago, Man crossed the Mediterranean by the shortest sea route from Africa to Gibraltar, where, even at the lowest sea levels, there would have been a 6-mile-wide channel (Clarke and Piggott, 1976, 41).

From theoretical considerations (Table 1) the only form of water transport in use at this early date would have been log floats.

Middle Palaeolithic (*c* 200 000 BC to *c* 40 000 BC)
During the later Middle Pleistocene and earlier Upper Pleistocene, *Homo sapiens neanderthalensis* and

Table 1   Theoretical earliest technological stage for floats, rafts and boats
Sources: Birdsell, 1977; Clark, 1977; Clark & Piggott, 1976; Johnstone, 1976; Keeley, 1980; *Somerset Levels Papers*, 1976, 1977.
Notes:
1 Evidence for earliest use of raw materials is usually indirect.
2 Evidence is probably distorted due to differential survival, e.g. reed/stone.
3 Before rafts or boats could be used purposefully, methods of propulsion and steering would need to be devised.
4 The table is based on the simplest version of each type of water transport.

Stage of technology	Tools	Earliest use of comparable raw materials	Earliest use of comparable techniques	Theoretical earliest stage at which construction of water transport possible		
				Floats	Rafts	Boats
Lower Palaeolithic	Flake tools Choppers Hand axes and cleavers	Branches Skins Reeds	Wood worked Skins used Reed gathered	Log		
Middle Palaeolithic	Scrapers Points, knives, some handaxes					
Upper Palaeolithic	Blades, awls and burins Bone and Antler tools including awls and needles	Bark strips	Binding Sewing skins	Reed	Reed Bark Log	Skin (frameless)
Upper Palaeolithic or Mesolithic		Bark sheet	Remove skin without slitting, or sew water-tight seam. Controlled heating	Skin	Buoyed	Bark
Mesolithic	Wedge and Hammer Axe Adze	Logs	Hollow log Woven basketry			Skin (with frame) Log
Neolithic	Ground stone tools		Coiled basketry Fashion simple planks Potting Treenail fastenings	Pot		See page 14
Bronze Age	Wide range of mould-produced tools	Bitumen Resin Moss etc.	Waterproof reeds Sew bark Fashion complex planks Sew planking Draw-tongue joints			Reed boats Multi-part bark boats Complex logboats Sewn planked boats

early *Homo sapiens* extended settlement further into Siberia, China and Japan (connected at that time to the mainland). Rafts and boats suitable for inland waterways would have facilitated these movements, but Table 1 indicates no change from the log floats available from earlier times.

Upper Palaeolithic (c 40 000 BC to c 8000 BC) During the final stages of the Pleistocene, Upper Palaeolithic Man (*Homo sapiens sapiens*) built upon the cultural foundations of Neanderthal Man and extended his domain over the north European plain as far as Denmark and along the rivers flowing across Siberia to the Arctic Ocean. Near the beginning of this period, possibly as early as 30 000 BC, Man crossed from north east Siberia to Alaska, subsequently to occupy the American continent. A sea level only 35 m lower than today's would convert the Bering Strait into a land bridge (Clark, 1977, 353) but a sea crossing via the Aleutian Islands or from Chukchi to Seward cannot be entirely ruled out (Johnstone, 1980, 5).

Some time before 30 000 BC, perhaps even before 40 000, Australia was first occupied by people from South-East Asia (Clark, 1977, 454–5, 461). Even at periods of lowest sea level there would have been stretches of water up to 80 km wide between Borneo (then joined to South-East Asia) and New Guinea (then linked to Australia) on the postulated northern route, or a maximum of 100 km to cross on a southern route via Java (front endpaper).

Table 1 suggests that during this period rafts of log, bark or reed, and frameless skin boats could have been used on inland waters, and possibly bark boats and buoyed rafts also. Rafts would have been suitable for crossing the warm seas between South-East Asia and Australia, but neither they nor frameless skin boats would seem appropriate for anything but a short sea crossing of the Bering Strait.

Mesolithic (c 8000 BC to c 7/4000 BC, depending on area) The ice sheets in northern Europe began their last retreat some 10 000 years ago with consequent environmental changes to which Man adapted. For example, the northern parts of the British Isles and the Scandinavian mainland and islands became available for settlement (Clark, 1977, 112–13), and large quantities of bones from deep-sea fish such as cod imply that water craft were used off the east and west coasts of Scotland and the west coast of Sweden by the 6th millenium BC (Clark, 1977, 112–14; Clark, 1952, 85).

Hollowed logs are known from this period: of these, the one found at Perth, Scotland, in the late 19th century is not dated with certainty to this period (McGrail, 1979B); and the hollowed pine log from Pesse, Netherlands, dated to c 6315 bc (Grn–486), is not unambiguously a boat (McGrail, 1978, 9). From theoretical considerations (Table 1) framed skin boats as well as logboats were technologically possible during the Mesolithic, as were all forms of raft. For seafishing and the colonisation of islands in northern waters the skin boat would probably have been the most appropriate.

Neolithic (c 7000 BC to c 2000 BC – precise duration depending on area) Neolithic cultures with their associated technology evolved from the Mesolithic as Man adapted to the Neothermal conditions of the post-Ice Age. This change began at varying times and progressed at varying speeds in different parts of Europe and Asia, but in general terms the Neolithic stage of technology was dominant in south-western Asia during the period c 7000 to 4000 BC and in northern Europe between c 4000 and c 2000 BC.

As the British islands had become separated by rising sea levels from continental Europe in the 7th millenium BC (Jacobi, 1976, 73), boats capable of carrying cattle would have been required to bring this element of the Neolithic economy from the Continent. Water transport would also have been essential for the occupation of such islands as Corsica and archipelagos such as Orkney. Axe blades made from rock quarried in Ulster have been found in Neolithic contexts in Britain implying the use of water transport, and similar deductions have been made about the movement of obsidian from the Mediterranean islands of Lipari and Sardinia in the 4th millenium BC (Hallam *et al.*, 1976; Camps, 1976; Ammerman, 1979).

Fifteen alder (*Alnus* sp.) logboats found during peat cutting in the Åmose bog, Verup, Denmark have been given a date of *c* 2000 BC by pollen analysis of the peat (Troels-Smith, 1946), but this dating method is insufficiently precise to decide whether these were of the Neolithic period or later. Two other Danish logboats and one French and one Italian have been given radiocarbon dates which fall within the later Neolithic or earlier Bronze Age (K-1473, 1649, 1650, 1651; Ly-792; R-359). None is published in detail. Remains of other forms of Neolithic water transport are not known, but some Norwegian rock carvings, possibly of this period, have been interpreted as representing skin boats (Clark, 1977, 147).

The planked boat is probably conceptually the most advanced form of early water transport and requires a wider and more developed array of tools and techniques. It therefore seems likely that it originated after other forms of water transport had been in use for some time. It is conceivable that during the Neolithic a simple form of planked boat – possibly similar to the South American *dalca* (p.80) – could have been built. However, no such boat of this date has been excavated, and Neolithic planks as at present known are not especially suitable for boat building.

Even if simple planked boats were in use in this period, skin boats might well have been a more sea-worthy alternative around Britain and Ireland and off western Scandinavia. For the Mediterranean, Johnstone (1980, 58) has suggested that reed rafts were likely. On inland waterways any of the available floats, rafts and boats (Table 1) could have been used, as appropriate to the varied natural environment in the regions of Europe and Asia. Although the use of reed rafts in prehistoric Ireland might at first sight seem unlikely, the fact that such craft were recently used on the River Suck in County Roscommon (Delaney, 1976) suggests that this possibility, and comparable ones elsewhere, should not be excluded.

Plate 9   The bow of a logboat found in Loch Arthur, Kirkcudbrightshire, and now in the National Museum of Antiquities, Edinburgh. Photo: NMM.

Later prehistoric Europe

This chapter deals mainly with northern and western Europe as the Mediterranean region is discussed in the second volume of this series.

The terms Bronze Age and Iron Age denote phases when the principal hand tools were made from these metals, but, as in the Stone Age, different regions in Europe could be at different technological stages. Thus, copper working appeared in Romania and Bulgaria in the early 4th millennium bc (Clark, 1977, 151); whereas for Britain, copper using probably began about the middle of the 3rd millennium bc. Greece acquired iron-working techniques c 1000 bc, and central Europe in the 7th century bc (Clark, 1977, 186–7); a date of 700 bc seems likely for Britain, and Clark (1977, 200) suggests 500 to 400 bc for Scandinavia. From c 300 BC Roman civilisation made its influence increasingly felt in Europe with significant effects on technology.

The Mediterranean

The evidence from the Egyptian, Phoenician, Greek and Roman civilisations is greater than for other areas, and iconographic and documentary evidence can be integrated with that from the few excavated boats and ships. The picture which emerges, however, is somewhat unbalanced in that planked craft predominate and form is more fully documented than structural details.

The Bronze Age Mediterranean
EGYPT Boat-shaped reed rafts, propelled by paddles or by sail, and steered by side-rudders were in use by the second half of the 4th millenium BC (Casson, 1971, 11). During the 3rd millenium BC papyriform planked boats began to be used, although reed craft continued in use for some tasks for many centuries. These early planked boats had a keel-plank rather than a keel and were built in the shell sequence with flush-laid planking edge-joined by sewing, treenail, mortice and tenon, or double-dovetail clamps. The mid-3rd millenium BC Cheops royal burial ship had crossbeams supported centrally by a longitudinal beam, as well as floor timbers, whereas the Dahshur boats of c 2000 BC had no floor timbers but numerous crossbeams. This may reflect differences of function or status rather than technological changes.

A distinctive feature in some of the larger ships was the hogging truss, a rope cable from bow to stern, keeping the shell pre-stressed. The mast was usually bipod, supported by forestay and backstays, with a single rectangular sail, and whilst some vessels had a single steering oar others, of papyriform shape, had two.

THE AEGEAN AREA The evidence, almost all documentary or iconographic, is principally of planked boats, although in view of the recent use of reed rafts in the Mediterranean (Johnstone, 1980, 12, 60) it seems possible that these, and perhaps other basic types, were also in use at an early date. Casson (1963) has deduced from documentary evidence that the earliest form of planked boat probably had sewn planking.

From c 2000 BC in the Middle Bronze Age, mast, rigging and sail are shown on ships carved on Minoan gems (Casson, 1971, 33). One end of these ships in longitudinal section is much higher than the other, but there is no agreement as to whether this represents a high bow or stern (both are known ethnographically): possibly two types are represented. In the Later Bronze Age from *c* 1600 BC, representations have two high ends and a vestigial 'ram' appears. Only a little planking survived from the Cape Gelidonya wreck of *c* 1200 BC (Bass, 1972, 24), but enough was recovered to show that the planks were edge-joined within their thickness by wooden treenails.

Iron Age Mediterranean

Classical techniques for building planked craft varied through time and place and because of differing uses ('longship' or 'roundship'), nevertheless a general method seems to emerge (but see Tchernia (1978) for an example of different techniques).

Although rivercraft might have flat, keel-less bottoms, seagoing ships had keel and stems, and were shell-built with flush-laid planking joined by draw-tongued joints within the thickness of the wood, generally with treenails through the tenons. Planking was pine, fir, cypress or cedar, with some elm below water. Close-set floor timbers, generally of oak, were fastened to the planking by treenails which in some ships had a copper nail driven through them. Wales and sometimes stringers gave longitudinal strength to the structure. Tarred fabric covered by lead was fastened by copper tacks to the underwater hull of some vessels as protection against marine borers.

Bronze Age northern and western Europe

By the Bronze Age, northern European man was technologically capable of building all the basic types of water transport including planked craft of complex form. Only logboats and planked boats have been excavated, but there is some slight representational evidence for skin boats.

Skin boats   Rock carvings in Scandinavia and northern Russia include some which probably represent water transport but there has been much discussion about dating and the precise types depicted (Coles and Harding, 1979, 317). In contrast to the skin boat theories of Marstrander (1963, 1976) and Johnstone (1972), Christensen (1972A, 161) believes some of these carvings (dated to the Bronze Age because they also appear on early metal swords) represent logboats or planked craft, and similarities with the Iron Age Hjortspring planked boat (see below) support his interpretation. On the other hand, some carvings (e.g. the Navestad group illustrated by Marstrander, 1963, Plate 64, figs.15 to 17), have an unusually low length/depth ratio, and thus may represent skin boats rather than planked craft. The only other possible evidence is the Caergwrle shale boat model from Flint, which is generally dated to this period and may represent a skin boat (Denford and Farrell, 1980). Evidence for Bronze Age skin boats is thus very meagre.

Logboats   A wooden model with figures from Roos Carr, Yorkshire, is thought to be from the Bronze Age and may represent a logboat with animal head and oculi at one end (front cover). This 'head' is comparable with the one on a logboat from Loch Arthur (Lotus), Kirkcudbright (Plate 9), recently dated to the 1st/2nd centuries BC (SRR-403).

Several European logboats have been dated by radiocarbon assay to the Bronze Age (McGrail, 1978). Of the British ones, the remains from Branthwaite and Chapel Flat Dyke are not indisputably logboats; but those from Locharbriggs, Dumfriesshire, dated to *c* 1804 bc (SRR-326), Appleby, Lincolnshire (*c* 1100 bc. Q-80); Short Ferry, Lincolnshire (*c* 846 bc. Q-79) and Brigg, Lincolnshire (*c* 834 bc. Q-78) undoubtedly are. All these logboats were of oak, built by variants of a standard method I have described elsewhere (McGrail, 1978). They may occasionally have been used as 'war canoes', but their more important uses would have been as ferries and for fishing, fowling, the transport of reeds and other materials. The biggest and the best documented of the British logboats was the one from Brigg, found in 1886 during excavations for a gas works near the River Ancholme and destroyed in a fire at Hull in 1941 (Plate 8). The log from which this boat was made was c 15 m in length with a diameter varying from 1.72 m to at least 1.90 m. Ninety per cent of this log had been worked away to produce a boat 14.8 m in length, 1.29–1.37 m in breadth and 1.00 m deep at the stern. Calculations indicate that this boat could have carried 2 men standing and 26 kneeling with a draft of only 0.36 m: that is, with a full crew, she could float in only 15 inches of water. With a 5-man crew and a cargo of over 10000 kg of stone the draft would be 0.88 m with a freeboard of 0.12 m. Compared with other logboats the Brigg boat had a first-rate capability as a carrier of high density cargo, and she was capable of comparatively good speed when propelled by 28 paddlers. Similar assessments may be made for other logboats (McGrail, 1978).

An analysis of the dated English and Welsh logboats shows that the following woodworking techniques were used during the Bronze Age:
Rectangular, sub-rectangular and flared transverse sections;
Fitted transom in a groove near the stern;
Integral ridges across the bottom;
Holes to gauge the thickness of the bottom;
Splits repaired by sewing, by cleat-patches or by flat double dovetailed tenons;
Moss caulking; and
Oculi.
And possibly:
Transverse strengthening fittings across the ends;
Longitudinal stabilisers or washstrakes; and
The use of treenails to fasten fittings.

Planked craft　Christensen (1972A, 161) believes that planked boats may be represented on some Scandinavian rock carvings – see also Hale (1980) – but the most significant evidence comes from Britain. Remains of three sewn-plank boats were found on the foreshore of a tidal stretch of the River Humber at North Ferriby, Yorkshire, and excavated by E.V.Wright and colleagues between 1937 and 1946, and in 1963 (Wright, 1976). Boats 1 and 2 are now in the reserve collection of the National Maritime Museum at Greenwich, whilst Boat 3 is in Hull Museum. Samples from these three boats have been dated by radiocarbon assay (Q-1197; Q-1217; Q-837; Q-715) to the mid-second millennium BC: they are thus the oldest known planked boats in Europe. Boat 1, with the most substantial remains (Plate 10), consists of the greater part of the bottom of the boat – 13.30 m out of an estimated 15.35 m – plus part of one side strake, the ends and the majority of the topsides having been dismantled in antiquity or been destroyed by natural effects. Her three oak bottom planks were stitched together with withy bindings of yew and the seams made watertight by a caulking of moss held in position by longitudinal oak laths. The planks were also connected laterally by transverse timbers through horizontal holes in cleats which had been left proud of each plank when it was hewn from its parent half-log. These planks are up to 650 mm in breadth and 140 mm thick and E.V.Wright (1976, 22) has calculated that the parent log must have had a minimum diameter of 1.10 m.

The most-likely original form and structure of Ferriby boat 1 is shown in Plate 11, a 1:10 scale model. This is a flat-bottomed boat with two side strakes, the ends being closed by watertight transoms. Internal support is given by three composite ribs set into projections from the bottom planks and lashed to side cleats, and by crossbeams (usable as thwarts) notched over the top strakes. A packing of withies held in the bottom of the boat by longitudinal laths would restrict movement of bilge water and

protect the stitching. These long and relatively narrow boats were probably used as ferries in the Humber estuary and its tributaries, propelled by paddle, or by pole in the shallows.

A related boat, the Brigg 'raft', was found in 1888 near the Ancholme, a tributary of the Humber, at Brigg in north Lincolnshire (McGrail, 1975): part of the remains was lifted, the remainder being re-interred. The 'raft' was re-excavated in 1974 by the National Maritime Museum and proved to be the bottom of a flat-bottomed boat with features related to the Ferriby boats: sewn oak planks with moss caulking and longitudinal laths at the plank seams, and transverse timbers through cleats left proud of the planking (Plate 12). Six planks were found in the 1974 excavation, five of them about 9 m long and 450 mm broad and one only *c* 150 mm broad. The 1888 records indicate that the planks were then 13 m in length. Holes on the outer edges of the outside planks show that further planking was once fastened there; the sixth (less substantial) plank was probably the lowest element of side planking. The ends of the boat were incomplete when found but it seems likely that this was a barge or punt-shaped boat. Owing to the disturbance of the remains in 1888, the precise method of ensuring a watertight joint between the planks is not now clear, but it cannot have been as effective as the interlocking joints used in the Ferriby boats. Thus it seems that the Brigg craft was more suitable for rivers than estuaries. Radiocarbon dates

Plate 10   Ferriby boat 1 during excavation from the River Humber foreshore in 1946. Photo: E.V. Wright.

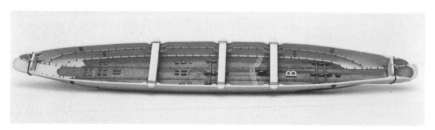

Plate 11   A 1:10 hypothetical reconstruction model of Ferriby boat 1. The parts in black represent elements which were excavated. Photo: NMM.

indicate that the 'raft' was in use around 650 bc. On Bradley's timescale (1978, 97) this would be Iron Age; however, it seems best to discuss it with its near neighbours, topographically and technologically, the Ferriby boats, although separated from them in time by 1000 years or so.

It is not possible to quantify the performance of the Brigg 'raft', but there is more evidence for the Ferriby boats, and using the minimum solution for Boat 1 (Plate 11) John Coates has calculated that with a load of 3 tonnes (crew and cargo) the freeboard would be 0.36 m and the draft 0.30 m. In fair weather it is thought that a maximum load of 5.5 tonnes could be carried with a freeboard of 0.26 m.

These four planked boats display woodworking techniques additional to those known from logboats: planks with regularly shaped cleats and morticed holes fashioned from half-logs; planks curved in two planes; and watertight joints involving interlocking planks sewn together.

Johnstone (1976) has drawn attention to the use of treenails, mortice and tenons and other joints to fasten together the elements of mid-third millennium wheels in southern Russia (Clark, 1977, 141). Treenails were probably used in the Bronze Age Appleby logboat (McGrail, 1978, 333), but mortice and tenon fastenings are not yet known in northern boats of this period.

Iron Age northern and western Europe (to c 400 AD)

Log rafts   Caesar recorded that the Celts used rafts to cross the River Rhine; two log rafts of simple

Plate 12   A stereophotogrammetric contour plot of the Brigg 'raft' during excavation in 1974. Drawing: Department of Photogrammetry, University College, London.

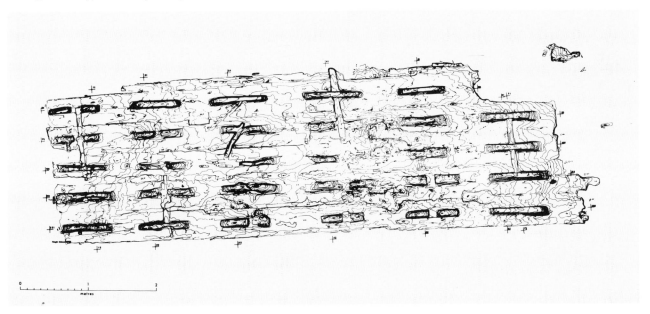

design and dated to the 2nd century AD were found in 1938 during canal work at Strasbourg–Köningshafen, France (Elmers, 1972, 22).

Skin boats   Several Roman authors, including Caesar and Pliny, described British boats of wicker framework covered with hides. They are also mentioned in the extracts from the 6th century BC *Massaliote Periplus* used by Avienus in his 4th century AD *Ora Maritima*. Although there are difficulties in identifying the place names it seems probable that this *Periplus* describes skin boat voyages in the seas between Brittany, Britain and Ireland (Hawkes, 1975). References to skin boats on the River Po by Lucan and in northern Spain by Strabo show that their use was not restricted to northern waters.

A small gold model boat from Broighter, County Derry, is dated by association to the 1st century BC (Plate 13). The model, now in the National Museum, Dublin, originally had 9 rowing thwarts with associated oar grommets through holes in the hull. Mast and yard indicate that she could also be sailed, and she appears to have been steered by an oar over the quarter. It is not certain which type of boat is represented but a skin boat, possibly a currach, seems likely (Farrell and Penny, 1975). The only other reference to excavated material is by Sheppard (1926) who noted a 'coracle-type vessel' containing a skeleton found near the mouth of the River Ancholme in north Lincolnshire and possibly of Roman date: the remains no longer survive.

Logboats   Ellmers (1978) has identified a 5th century BC gold model from Dürnberg as that of a logboat-based craft: the pivoted oars on this model are the first indication of their use in northern Europe. Roman authors mention the use of logboats in Spain, France, Germany, central Europe and the Black Sea. Their recent use in such places as Albania, Estonia, and Russia may indicate wide use in earlier times.

Five logboats from Britain have been dated to this period: Shapwick from the 3rd to 5th century BC (Q-357); Poole (Q-821) and Holme-Pierrepont 1 (Birm-132) from the 3rd or 4th century BC; L.Arthur (Lotus) from the 1st or 2nd century BC (SRR-403); and Hardham 2 from the 3rd or 4th century AD (Q-827). Logboats or similar wooden containers have also been dated to this period from France (four between *c* AD 100 and *c* AD 500), Italy (three between *c* AD 130 and *c* AD 500), and Sweden (two from *c* 535 bc and 265 bc). Although no radiocarbon dates have yet been published, three oak logboats excavated at Zwammerdam, Netherlands, from a site on the former south bank of the River Rhine appear to be dated by associated material to the period AD 150–225 (de Weerd, 1978, 15). Boat 1 and boat 5 have the midship section of their hulls pierced to form a fishwell between watertight bulkheads.

Plate 13   Gold model boat from Broighter, Co. Derry, Ireland. Photo: National Museum of Ireland.

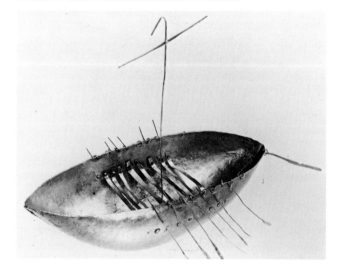

Boat 3, of flared transverse section with washstrakes, has paired, alternating half-ribs iron-nailed to the hull and a small (towing) mast-step. Two logboats excavated from a site at Pommeroeul near the River Haine, a tributary of the Rhine, in Belgium and provisionally dated to the 1st/2nd centuries AD (de Boe, 1978), also have paired alternating half-ribs.

Analysis of the five British logboats shows that the following woodworking techniques were in use, in addition to those for which there is evidence from the Bronze Age:

Half-rounded transverse section;
'Steps' fashioned inside one end; and
Lead repair patches nailed on.

The fashioning of a non-functional stem on the Poole logboat indicates that by this time (c 295 bc), if not earlier, southern Britons were familiar with planked craft with stems.

Planked craft   The planked boats of this region dated to the period c 500 BC to AD 400 may be discussed under four headings.

CENTRAL EUROPEAN BOATS   The remains of a flat-bottomed boat, some 30 m in length and with a maximum beam of c 4.50 m reducing to c 2 m towards the ends, were found in 1890 on the bed of a former lake near the town of Ljubljana in Yugoslavia (formerly Laibach, Austria). From stratigraphic and documentary evidence Müllner (1892) deduced that the boat was deposited between 500 and 100 BC, a date compatible with the iron nails used in the construction.

The form and structure of the ends could not be recorded, but the excavator (Müllner, 1892) noted that the spruce bottom planks were caulked with lime bast and fastened together with lime bast rope through holes 80–100 mm apart by continuous double stitching. Forty-two elm floor timbers were fastened to the flat bottom of the boat by vertical buckthorn treenails. These timbers were notched at the plank joins in such a manner that caulking and sewing of the planking could have taken place before or after they had been fitted: which sequence was used is unclear from the surviving records. In between the floor timbers were oak knees worked from crooks and fastened to the bottom planking by vertical treenails. To their upper arms were treenailed three strakes to a height of 0.50 m. This side planking was caulked and sewn together before the knees were fitted. The planks at the transition from bottom to sides had a concave cross section, similar to, but not so complex as, the side strake on Ferriby boat 1. Four longitudinal timbers of elm were fastened by vertical treenails and dome-headed, square cross-section, iron nails to the planking and to the floor-timbers or knees. The iron nails passed through the caulking where the planks met, and were turned at right angles underneath the planking, thereby fastening the longitudinal timber through the floor timbers to the planking and also trapping the caulking at these points.

This boat thus had similarities with the Ferriby and Brigg boats with flat bottom, sewn planking, and probable shell sequence, but was technologically more advanced in having cleat-less planking, sturdier floor timbers, knees, longitudinal timbers, and some metal fastenings.

Fragments of another sewn boat have recently been recovered from an underwater site near Nin, Yugoslavia, and are thought to be 1st–3rd century AD (Brusic, 1968). Flush-laid planks were sewn to the keel and to each other by liana; the holes were wedged and the outboard part of the stitch cut away. No caulking is reported but a lath under the stitches covered the seams, which were further waterproofed with resin.

SCANDINAVIAN BOATS   During excavation at Hjortspring on the Island of Als, Denmark, the remains of a round bottom, sewn-plank boat were found in what had formerly been a small lake. This find has been dated to c 350–300 BC by reference to the associated weapons. The hull of limewood was built of seven parts: a bottom plank, four side-planks and two end pieces. The bottom plank extended beyond the end pieces and was continued by an upward-curving timber. The end pieces (block-stems) were morticed and sewn to the bottom plank and had 'wings' of plank thickness to which were stitched two side planks each side. The end pieces also had timber projections parallel to the bottom plank extensions. At each end these two projections were joined by a vertical timber of oak fitting into mortices. The upper strakes overlapped the lower strakes by c 20 mm in a bevelled lap (Greenhill, 1976, fig.26) so that there was little, if any, change in thickness. Lime bast cord was used to fasten the planking through small holes outside the lap and at c 70–80 mm intervals; the holes were then stopped with resin. Details of the sewing are only known from marks left in this resin, and Prins (personal communication) believes that individual lashings may have been used rather than continuous stitching. Hazel branches bent to the curve of the boat and lashed to perforated cleats proud of each plank ran from upper strake to upper strake. These flexible hazel ribs were thus clamping the planks together like an arch. Further support was provided by transverse ash timbers at lower strake level and upper transverse lime timbers which doubled as thwarts. Two vertical ash timbers linked each rib to the upper timbers. The boat was propelled by 20 double-banked paddlers, and steered from either end by a steering oar. It is estimated that she was originally c 13.61 m in length (without projections), 2.04 m maximum beam and 0.71 m deep amidships.

This is thus the oldest known boat with overlapping strakes and, although the overlap is unusual, the boat may be considered as a forerunner of the Scandinavian clinker-built boats. It is not clear from the published reports whether the curve of the side planking was due to hewing or to bending: if this could be established the boat's position in the development of boatbuilding could more clearly be seen.

In 1971 a group of Danes built a replica of this find based on Johannesen's reconstruction drawings (Rosenberg, 1937). Lime timber of the dimensions originally used was unobtainable, thus the replica was less deep and significantly less broad than the original. The Danes found their boat easy to paddle and responsive to the steering oar. Ballast was required to achieve stability but, owing to the replica's lack of breadth, this is probably not a true reflection of the original boat's performance.

In 1896 fragments of a planked boat were excavated from a moss in Halsnøy, Søndhordland, Norway (Shetelig, 1903). The pine planking was fastened with root lashings with a 'Scandinavian' style clinker overlap (Greenhill, 1976, fig.26), the sewing being within the lap and the stitches countersunk into the timber on the outboard side. The ribs, which were grown timber crooks (and thus in Horridge's (1978) terms 'stiff' load-carrying members), were fastened to cleats on the planking, and a thole timber was lashed to the top strake. From typological considerations Brøgger and Shetelig (1971, 39) date this boat to c 200 AD. No independent method of dating has been attempted.

ROMANO–CELTIC BOATS Caesar (*De Bello Gallico*, 3.13) and Strabo (4.195) described the sea-going ships of the Veneti, a Celtic people of north-west France, as broad and flat-bottomed with high bow and stern, oak planking caulked with seaweed and thick transverse timbers fastened with stout nails. Leather sails were used but not oars. Features appear to be mentioned in contrast to Roman practices, thus we may deduce that the planking was flush-laid rather than clinker. These Veneti ships were evidently more suited to local conditions than those of the Romans, and could enter shallows and take the ground better.

Muckelroy *et al.* (1978) believe that a ship on an early 1st century AD Celtic coin excavated in Canterbury, Kent, may have some of the features described by Caesar. The ship has mast and yard, stays and possibly braces. A horizontal projection from the bottom of one end is thought to represent a protruding forefoot to facilitate beaching.

Aspects of Caesar's description may also be seen in a group of a dozen or so boats of barge form, recently excavated mostly from the Rhine region, and dated to the 1st to 3rd centuries AD (Plate 14). These finds are from the Netherlands: Zwammerdam boats, 2, 4 and 6 (de Weerd, 1978), Kapel Avezaath (de Weerd, 1978, 15) and Druten (Lehmann, 1978); from Belgium: Pommeroeul boats 1 and 2 (de Boe, 1978); from Switzerland: Yverdon and Bevaix (Arnold, 1978); from France: Abbeville (Arnold, 1978); and from London: Blackfriars boat 1 and New Guys House (Marsden, 1976). More fragmentary remains are from Bruges, Belgium (Marsden, 1976) and Avenches, Switzerland (Arnold, 1978). Some of the published descriptions leave questions unanswered. Nevertheless a partial attribute analysis may be undertaken. Significant features include:

1 Flat keel-less bottom with flush-laid planking which was generally not edge-joined (Pommeroeul 2 was edge-joined).

2 The transition strakes between bottom and sides generally had an L-shaped or rounded cross section (Blackfriars 1 did not have this feature).

3 The form of the bottom of these boats, where not flat, appears to have been determined by the shape of the floor timbers; where there were rising ends the shape was obtained by bending the planking. The run of Blackfriar's 1 side planking (and possibly New Guy's House) was initially determined by the shape

of the floor timber ends, and subsequently by the shape of pre-erected side timbers. On the other hand, it is possible that in the other craft the transverse curve of the transition strake between bottom and sides determined the form of the sides, the ends of the floor timbers being made to fit. Thus alternative sequences of building are possible: further details are required before this matter can be decided.

4 Floor timbers fastened to planking by iron nail clenched by turning. In Blackfriars 1 and Bruges these nails were driven through treenails piercing the

Plate 14   Zwammerdam boat 6 during excavation by the Instituut voor Prae-en Protohistorie. Photo: University of Amsterdam.

floor timbers. Not all nails in the Zwammerdam and Bevaix craft pierce the timbers. The floor timbers may be single or paired. In two boats with single timbers there is an average of 2.5 timbers per metre of length; in two with paired timbers this figure is 1.6: this may indicate boats intended to carry cargoes of different density. The floor timbers are generally L-shaped (not Blackfriars 1) with the vertical arms on alternate sides of the boat: associated side timbers may be fastened on the side opposite to the vertical arm.

5 L/B ratio in the range 5.9 to 8.1 (six examples).
6 L/D ratio in the range 21.5 to 28.3 (six examples).
7 Several boats have a mast step (probably for towing): most are in a transverse timber but Zwammerdam 2 has one in a longitudinal timber.
8 Blackfriars 1, New Guy's House and possibly Druten appear to have had stems, whereas the other boats were probably square-ended.
9 Some of the boats with transition strakes also had washstrakes, but some did not: some washstrakes were overlapping, but some were flush. In general they were fastened to the arms of floor timbers and side timbers, but in parts of Zwammerdam 6 they were edge-fastened by draw-tongue joints, and possibly by nails.
10 A variety of caulking materials were used – hazel, twigs, twisted fibres, moss. In the Bevaix and Yverdon boats the caulking was kept in place by laths nailed along the seams: details of the other craft are not available.

These boats, whilst not identical, share sufficient characteristics to be considered a group, 'Romano-Celtic', distinguishable from the contemporary boatbuilding traditions in Scandinavia and the Mediterranean. Variability in certain attributes may be as expected in such a polythetic group (Doran & Hodson, 1975, 160). On the other hand the variability may be due to differences of function or to changes over time, or even indicate significant local traditions. These possibilities can be investigated further when details and measured drawings have been published for all the finds.

The transition strakes on these boats are sometimes said to have been constructed from a logboat split in half longitudinally. A priori it is unlikely that a log would be hollowed and then split: a more economical way would be to fashion the curved plank from a half-log, and there is a tradition of hewing planks this way in northern Europe extending back to the Iron Age Ljubljana boat and the Bronze Age Ferriby boats. The split logboat theory might receive some support from dendrological examination of the timber, but there are no reports that this has been undertaken.

THE MEDITERRANEAN TRADITION   A few finds from north-west Europe display woodworking techniques similar to those on Roman Age wrecks from the Mediterranean. Of these, the County Hall ship excavated from the south bank of the Thames in 1910 is dated by associated coins to after AD 293 (Riley, 1912). This flat-bottomed, rounded-bilge oak vessel had a shallow keel and was built in shell sequence with flush-laid planking edge-fastened at c 6 in. (150 mm) intervals by draw-tongued joints pierced by $\frac{5}{8}$ in. diameter treenails; there was no sign of caulking. The 7th strake was extra thick and slotted to take crossbeams. Alternate floor timbers were extended by side timbers. Floor and side timbers were fastened to the planking, but not to the keel, by $1\frac{1}{4}$ in. treenails and some iron spikes. Longitudinal timbers on either side of the keel were let into the floor timbers and fastened by iron spikes. Morticed holes in them were probably for upright stanchions to support crossbeams. The form of the ends could not be determined but the ship is estimated to have been c 60 ft in length with a beam of c 16 ft.

Fir planking of boat 2A from Zwammerdam (de

Weerd and Haalebos, 1973) was connected in a similar manner to that of the County Hall ship with oak joints at intervals of *c* 180mm. Similar joints were also found fastening a washstrake edge-to-edge with the transition strake on Zwammerdam boat 6, and also joining together the three parts of a steering oar from the same site (de Weerd, 1978). A boat excavated in Vechten, Utrecht, Netherlands, in 1893, and dated by associated material to the 1st century AD, also appears to have had this type of joint at intervals of *c* 120mm (de Weerd and Haalebos, 1973).

The County Hall ship was probably built in the Roman tradition. On the other hand, Zwammerdam boat 6 was 'non-Roman' except for this use of draw-tongued joints, which may thus be a secondary feature. Insufficient remains of Zwammerdam boat 2A were found for other features to be recorded.

Continuity into the medieval period

We cannot yet be certain of the range of water transport in use during the final phase of the western Roman Empire but log (and possibly reed) rafts, skin boats, logboats and a variety of planked boats had been used during the previous 1000 years somewhere in Europe: there is thus the possibility of their continued use. Some types may have been restricted to inland waterways, but seagoing skin boats are documented, and although rafts are unlikely to have been used in northern seas they are known to have been used in the Mediterranean (Casson, 1971, 5). Logboats may be seagoing if their stability is increased (by expansion, by stabilisers or by pairing) and their freeboard increased by washstrakes. Stabilisers and paired logboats may have been in use in the pre-medieval period, but there is no evidence for expansion.

Planked boats and ships in use from the mid-first millennium BC may be listed under four headings,

using some of the general attributes of form and structure:

1 Flat-bottomed; generally keel-less; flush-planking edge-fastened by sewing; probably shell sequence (Brigg, Ljubljana, River Nin).
2 Flat-bottomed; keel-less; generally not edge-fastened; probably non-shell sequence ('Romano-Celtic').
3 Round-hulled or flat-bottomed; keel-less or keeled; flush-planking edge-fastened generally by wood; generally shell sequence (Classical Mediterranean).
4 Round-hulled; keel-less; overlapping planking edge-fastened by sewing; shell sequence (Scandinavian).

These groupings must be considered provisional. It could be that 1 and 2 are different phases of the same tradition, or that 1, 2 and 3 each include more than one tradition; such possibilities must await detailed attribute analysis and further finds for support or refutation. Of these groups: 1 was for inland waterways; some of 2 and 3 were seagoing; and 4 was probably restricted to sheltered inshore waters.

Sail was in use in the Mediterranean from at least 2000 BC (Casson, 1971, 31) and Pytheas' voyage in *c* 325 BC (Hawkes, 1975, 44) would probably have made this known in northern Europe if not known there already. It has been claimed that some of the prehistoric Scandinavian rock carvings show sail, but the generally held view is that this is not so (Schovsbo, 1980). The only examples of indigeneous sail in northern waters during the prehistoric period are the Broighter boat model of the 1st century BC with mast and yard, and Caesar's Veneti description. Ellmers (1969, 81, Plate 61) has deduced from representations on gravestones that Celtic sails of the 2nd/3rd century AD were rectangular, of high aspect ratio, with two horizontal battens and a boom at the foot.

Medieval Europe to AD 1400

Evidence for the medieval period is available from a wider range of sources than for earlier times. On the other hand, it is only occasionally possible to relate type names given in medieval documents to excavated remains and iconographic representations, and thus these sources of evidence cannot always be integrated. As with the prehistoric period, the available medieval material is biased towards the logboats and planked boats of north and west Europe. It is convenient to include here the bark and skin boats of northern and eastern U.S.S.R.

Non-planked craft

Reed rafts   Rafts of reed (Plate 15) are known to have been in use recently on inland waterways in western Ireland (Delaney, 1976); Hungary and Sardinia (Brindley, 1931, 12, 15); and seagoing ones from Corfu (Johnstone, 1980, 60). It seems likely, but cannot be demonstrated, that in earlier times they were in widespread use where suitable reeds grew.

Log rafts   Ellmers has described three north European, early medieval rafts of parallel logs linked by transverse members. Similar simple structures were in use on the River Isar at Munich and on the Danube in the late 15th century (Ellmers, 1972, 106–7). Early use elsewhere is probable, but has not been documented.

Bark boats   Bark boats are known to have been used from at least the 19th century in eastern Siberia (Brindley, 1919, 66–7, 104–7) for river and estuary fishing and hunting. Brindley's description implies

that the bark was sewn (by leather thongs) to a pre-erected wooden framework, but this deduced sequence may only be due to his phraseology. Bark boats cannot be shown to have been used in earlier times, although Ellmers (1972) notes undated bark remains found at Istorp, Sweden and Lauvasvik, Norway.

Skin boats   There are contemporary references in Irish, British and Anglo-Saxon chronicles to the use of skin boats in the waters between Britain and Ireland from the 5th to the 9th century. They are also mentioned in 7th century accounts of the life of Saint Columcille, 10th century accounts of Saint Brendan, and 12th century accounts of Ireland and Wales by Giraldus Cambrensis. These boats had a wicker or osier framework covered by cowhides tanned in oak bark, with a single mast and sail, and were generally similar to those recently used in Ireland and Wales as described by James Hornell (1970, 133–48). An 8th century carving on a pillar at Bantry, County Cork, has been identified as that of a skin boat of currach, boat-shaped form (Johnstone, 1964). The only excavated evidence comes from a late 10th century crannog site at Ballinderry, County Westmeath, where a 1.27 m length of timber has been interpreted as a currach's top stringer with small holes 90 mm apart to hold the ends of the transverse osier framework (Ellmers, 1972).

Whether Saint Brendan or other early medieval Irishmen reached America is disputed, but there can be little doubt that Irishmen had settled in Iceland and other northern islands by the early 8th century

(Taylor, 1971, 70; Jones, 1964, 102). These were probably the first recorded voyages in northern waters necessarily made out of sight of land, and although early medieval Irishmen knew of, and indeed used, planked boats (Anderson, 1961), it is likely that these ocean voyages were made in seagoing skin boats. The seagoing qualities of such craft were demonstrated during Severin's voyage across the Atlantic via Iceland in a 36 ft skin boat built by traditional Irish methods. This craft proved to have considerable stability and remained relatively dry in rough Atlantic seas. After six months afloat the frame had lost some sheer and the skin of 42 cowhides had developed corrugations, otherwise the boat was in good shape. With two square sails she had a cruising speed of 2–3 knots in winds up to Force 4 or 5. Severin (1978, 277) estimated that an experienced crew might average 40 to 60 miles a day. However, when attempting to beat to windward, the boat made considerable leeway with no headway when within 60° or 70° of the wind.

The *baidara* and *baidarka* of the Bering Strait and eastern Siberia are similar to North American skinboats (p.79). The *umiak* and *baidara* are large double-ended boats, deep-sided and flat-bottomed, propelled by oar or in favourable conditions by a square sail; whereas the *kayak* and *baidarka* are light, sharp-ended, decked-over boats propelled by double paddle, generally with a single crew. These skin boats were known to western Europeans from at least the 17th century, when a Danish expedition to north Russia captured a 2-man *kayak* (Johnstone, 1980, 220). Earlier reports by Claudius Clavis in 1430 and Olaus Magnus in 1505 may also refer to Russian skin boats. Commodore J. Billings (Sauer, 1802) described the building of a late 18th century *baidara* in Kamchatka: a framework of a keelson and three pairs of longitudinal stringers, linked by light floor timbers and knees lashed on with whales' fins, was

covered with animal hides. The boats were excellent surf boats, and were light (a 12-man boat could be carried by only 4 men) and drew only a few inches of water though carrying a considerable load. The smaller ones (*baidarka*) were covered over, leaving 1, 2 or 3 openings for the paddler(s). Their use in early Siberia cannot be documented, but seems likely.

Logboats   There is continuing, but sporadic evidence for logboats in medieval Europe and indeed well into post-medieval times. Boats from France, Norway, Russia, Sweden and Italy have been dated by radiocarbon to the period *c* ad 450–1300 and twelve logboats from Britain are dated between *c* ad 640 and ad 1335. There is no evidence for a fitted transom stern in the medieval period, otherwise the techniques of logboat building used in prehistoric Britain continued to be used until at least the 9th century AD. This may be evidence for long-surviving traditions; but it may be because features have been defined too broadly, allowing, for example, several different dovetail joints to be classified as one.

Plate 15   A reed raft with light wooden superstructure on the River Suck, County Roscommon, in 1962. Photo: National Museum of Ireland.

Eight of the eleven logboats recovered from the River Mersey between Warrington and Manchester have radiocarbon dates in the 9th to 12th centuries ad, and were probably in use in the 11th century ad (McGrail and Switsur, 1979). These boats are reasonably well documented and attribute analysis reveals that they have sufficient features in common to be considered a group with the following characteristics:

Short oaks with girths in proportion, were selected and split longitudinally. Maximum use was made of these half-logs by giving the boats a half-rounded transverse section and longitudinal taper in elevation and plan. The fashioning of rounded ends thus resulted in a 'canoe' form. Beaks with horizontal holes for a painter were left protruding from the bow end. Treenails were used to fasten fittings to the hull, and the holes for these and for thickness gauges were c 23–27 mm in diameter (i.e. 'one inch'). Ridges were left across the bottom at about one-third of the length from the ends of some of the boats. Transverse strengthening fittings—crooks naturally curved to the required shape—were fastened to the ends of the boats to minimise the risk of the log splitting. There were no fittings for propulsion by oar or by sail.

A small planked boat (Plate 16) excavated by Dr David Wilson (1966) in 1955 from the former lake of Kentmere, Westmorland, and now in the National Maritime Museum has a logboat base extended by five oak strakes, each consisting of two scarfed planks. The planking was supported by four grown birch ribs treenailed into position and longitudinal oak timbers were treenailed externally along the sides to act as stabilisers at the waterline. A pair of ash rowlocks were fastened to the upper strakes by treenails in association with a plank or thwart. A radiocarbon assay has given a date of c ad 1300, a salutary reminder that not all simple boat forms are early.

There are reasons for believing that this boat began as a basic logboat whose rotten or damaged sides were subsequently pared down and replaced by planks (McGrail, 1978, 330).

There are records of many logboats from continental Europe (Ellmers, 1972, 1973), many of them with fittings of great interest but few radiocarbon or tree ring dates have been published. Until these are available attribute analysis could be misleading as the boats may range in date from the Bronze Age to the 20th century AD. Several examples of logboats extended by washstrakes are thought to be medieval,

Plate 16　The after end of the 13th/14th century AD extended logboat excavated from Kentmere, Westmorland, in 1955. Photo: Dr David Wilson.

including that from Björke, Sweden which had also been extended at bow and stern (Ellmers, 1972). An extended logboat from Antwerp (Ellmers, 1972) appears to be 11th century AD. Nails clenched by turning fastened a longitudinal batten to the upper and lower washstrakes; the latter being fastened to the boat by treenails. Moss in the seams was capped by a lath held by iron clamps, a feature common to four planked boats found nearby (see below).

There are no medieval logboats unambiguously identified as expanded, although Crumlin-Pedersen (1972B) has argued that the Scandinavian planked boat tradition was developed from such craft. Ten logboats excavated from Novgorod, Russia, in 1899, dated stratigraphically to the 10th/11th centuries (Ellmers, 1972) appear to be similar in materials, form and fittings to 20th century expanded logboats from Estonia (Manninen, 1927) and Finland (Nikkilä, 1947) except that washstrakes were sewn rather than nailed: whether these Novgorod boats were expanded cannot now be determined.

Northern planked craft

Sewn boats   In the foreword to his catalogue of medieval boat and shipfinds in northern and central Europe, Ellmers (1972) drew attention to the problem of dating most of them other than by reference to a theory of technological development postulated as:

up to c 300 BC:	planking sewn; ribs lashed
300 BC–AD 400:	planking iron-nailed; ribs lashed
after AD 400:	planking nailed; ribs lashed and treenailed.

However, there are three finds from northern Norway which cannot be fitted into this technological framework: finds from Oksnes near Tromsø, Volkijärvi, Lapland and Skagen, Nordland combine sewn planking with treenailed ribs. Dating other than

by technological change must therefore be sought.

Ellmers (1972) describes ten sewn or partly-sewn planked boat finds, whilst Prins (personal communication) has recorded five others. Of these, four are from outside northern Scandinavia: Hjortspring (Denmark), Halsnøy (Hordaland, Norway), Hille (Gastrikland, Sweden) and one found at No.4, Skeppergaten in Stockholm; only Hjortspring has been dated by independent means and this is prehistoric. Of the northern ones, only that from Skagen (Nordland) can be dated and Ellmers (1972) gives this a pre-Viking date because of the associated runes. There are references in the sagas to sewn boats; Olaus Magnus describes early 16th century Lapp boats sewn with sinew (Johnstone, 1980, 24); and they have been noted by others off northern Scandinavia and Russia up to the present century (Plate 17). Two undated boats with planking sewn with fir roots were found near the River Hara and River

Plate 17   A 17th century drawing of a Lapp (?) sewn boat encountered by W. Barents off Nova Sembla (Novaya Zemlya, northern USSR) in c AD 1600. From de Bry, 1629, plate LVI.

Narva, Estonia in 1932 (Rank, 1933). Their seams were made waterproof by moss held in place by a lath fastened to the planking by metal clamp, comparable with the Bremen cog and other craft (see p.36). Rank quotes other undated finds of sewn boats in Lapland, Finland, the coastal Arctic and the Lake of Ladoga.

The use of lashings to fasten ribs to planking has been recorded on finds from Scandinavia and other Baltic countries (Ellmers, 1972; Brogger and Shetelig, 1971; Rank, 1933) ranging from Lapland to Schleswig-Holstein. Only Hjortspring, Nydam and the three ships from the Oslo Fjord burial mounds (see below) are dated by independent means.

In northern Scandinavia and Russia a sewn boat tradition seems to have persisted from prehistoric until recent times. Further south this tradition was probably superseded early in the medieval period, but with lashed ribs persisting until the 9th century AD. Thus an early date cannot be assumed for finds with sewn planking or with lashed ribs: dating by other means is required.

Proto-Viking boatbuilding   Six boat finds from the Pre-Viking period in Scandinavia and in England have features which may link the prehistoric Hjortspring find with boats and ships of the Viking Age. Fragments from Gretstedbro (AD 550 ± 100) and Hasnaes 1 (AD 590 ± 100) are dated by radiocarbon. The two Sutton Hoo boats (back cover) (early 7th/ late 6th century), the Snape boat (second half of 6th century) and Nydam boat 2 (second half 4th century) are dated by associated finds. Nydam boat 2 (23.70 × 3.75 × 1.20 m), now on display in the Schloss Gottorp Museum, Schleswig has shrunk since she was in use, but of the three attempts at theoretical reconstruction only Akerlund's (1963) appears to allow for this. The rowing geometry and the positioning of the side rudder remain to be in-

vestigated further. Elements of two other planked boats found in the same bog as Nydam 2 have not been dated. The Snape boat and the two Sutton Hoo boats survived in their burial mounds as patterns of nails and imprints of other features in the sand. A plaster mould was taken of the larger Sutton Hoo find (No.2) in 1967 and part of the resulting fibre-glass positive is now on display at the National Maritime Museum. Using the published reconstruction drawing (Bruce–Mitford, 1975) of Sutton Hoo 2 (27.15 m × 4.6 × 1.3) John Coates has calculated that with a draft of 0.71 m and a freeboard of 0.62 m she could have carried 60 men and 7 tonnes of equipment.

Systematic attribute analysis is not yet practicable but it is possible to record the change in, or persistence of, certain features. All these finds had clinker planking fastened by iron nails clenched over roves. Nydam 2 and Sutton Hoo 2 were shell-built, double-ended, with floor timbers fashioned from crooks installed symmetrically about the centre line c 1 m apart. They had relatively thin planking except for the top strake which was reinforced. The central bottom member was a keel-plank (broader than deep) rather than a keel and was fastened to the stems by horizontal scarfs. Nydam 2 had rabbetted stems and a side rudder, and Sutton Hoo 2 probably did also. Both boats were propelled by oars pivoted in grommets against single tholes and their length/breadth ratio was 6 or 7 to 1.

Other features changed between the 4th century Nydam 2 and the late 6th century Sutton Hoo 2: tholes were nailed rather than lashed; ribs were tree-nailed to the planking rather than lashed; there were more planks per strake; and the longitudinal sheer increased.

Remains of two other clinker built, iron nail-fastened boats, were found during peatcutting in 1920 at Kvalsund, Sunnmøre, Norway. The larger boat had a T-shaped keel almost as deep as broad, with a vertically projecting reinforcing fillet above it. The ribs were lashed to the lower planking and iron and treenailed to the upper. The sheer at the ends appears to have been more marked than in the Sutton Hoo boat. In these aspects and in her steering arrangements this boat was somewhat like the ships of the early Viking Age; however the keel/stem scarfs were reported to be horizontal like the proto-Viking boats. The smaller boat was similar in construction but had the ribs treenailed to the planking, unusually through integral cleats. These boats can only be dated by the dubious method of technological comparison, which places them between Nydam 2 and the Oseberg ship.

The Viking tradition   Much of the evidence for this tradition comes from Scandinavian wrecks and graves, in particular the 9th century Oseberg, Gokstad (Plate 18) and Tune burial ships and the five 10th/11th century ships used to block a channel of Roskilde Fjord at Skuldelev. In addition, there are wrecks from the eastern Baltic and a certain amount of information from such sites as Dublin and Orkney where the Vikings settled. The Icelandic sagas and the Anglo-Saxon Chronicles, when examined critically, also reveal something of Viking Age shipbuilding and use, and wood carvings, stone engravings and embroideries help to fill out the picture, especially in the matter of rigging.

From the period *c* AD 800 to 1200 there are about 30 finds sufficiently well-documented to contribute to our knowledge of boatbuilding technology. Fifteen of these were probably cargo carriers (Plate 19) as they have holds amidships or rowing stations only at the ends; or their length/breadth ratio is less than about 5 and length/depth ratio less than about 10; or their inter-frame distances are significantly less than 1 m; or in rare cases cargo was found in them. Eleven others were probably for carrying men: such craft

Plate 18   The Gokstad ship during excavation from the burial mound near Oslo in 1880. Photo: Universitetets Oldsaksamling.

Plate 19   A 1:10 model of cargo ship Skuldelev 3, as reconstructed. Photo: Ole Crumlin-Pedersen.

31

commonly have rowing positions the full length of the vessel, and a length/breadth ratio greater than 5: the larger ones were probably 'longships' (warships); the shorter ones ship's boats, ferries or fishing boats. The ships from Gokstad, Oseberg and Tune are difficult to classify and may be considered either as special craft built as 'royal yachts', or as general-purpose ships built before specialisation of function had developed. Crumlin-Pedersen (1969, 1972A, 1978) has shown that from these finds the characteristics common to ships and boats of the Viking tradition may be identified:

FORM   The hull was (almost) double-ended with a slightly rockered keel blending into curved stems. The sheerline had a distinctive curve with pronounced sheer towards the ends, and the transverse sections were characteristic with a rounded bottom and flared sides.

STRUCTURE   The hull was built in shell sequence with relatively thin clinker-laid strakes fastened to a 'backbone' of keel and stems, the keel being a rela-tively prominent one with a vertical scarf to the stems. Evenly-spaced, symmetrically-placed, floor timbers were lashed or treenailed to the planking but not to the keel, thus producing a strong, resilient structure. Fastened to every floor timber was a characteristically slender crossbeam, with a system of knees and upper crossbeams at some or all of these stations.

It is generally thought that fashioning and fitting planking was done by eye, based on tradition and inherited skill. However, the principal dimensions and the plank angles of a boat may be recorded in coded form and subsequently be used to check the form of another boat during building. Christensen (1972B) has identified two post-medieval Scandinavian aids, the boat-ell and the boat-level (Plate 20), which can be used in this way but there is at present no evidence for their earlier use. Temporary moulds may also be used to check the form of a boat and leave little trace, but on present evidence they do not seem to have been used in Viking times.

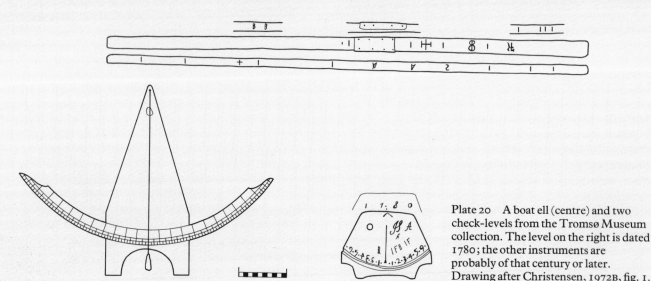

Plate 20   A boat ell (centre) and two check-levels from the Tromsø Museum collection. The level on the right is dated 1780; the other instruments are probably of that century or later. Drawing after Christensen, 1972B, fig. 1.

Boats were propelled by oars pivoted in grommets against single tholes on the sheerline or through oarports in an upper strake. Sailing craft also had a mast stepped (near) amidships with a rectangular sail. They were steered by a side-rudder usually over the starboard quarter.

There were certain changes in building techniques during the Viking period but these are difficult to date precisely. For example, some of the earlier ships (Gokstad, Oseberg, Tune of the 9th century) had rounded cross-section floor timbers lashed to the lower planking, whilst later finds had rectangular cross-section timbers fastened by treenails. However, the small boats found inside the Gokstad ship had the treenailing technique as did the Äskekärr find of the mid-9th century and some of the proto-Viking craft (see p.30 above). Crumlin-Pedersen (1969, 31) has tentatively suggested that changes in the positioning and number of crossbeams can be documented, enabling wrecks of cargo ships from the 10th to 13th century to be dated on typological grounds within narrow limits. But, further work on this topic and on changes in the mast support system, the several forms of scarf in use, and the introduction of stringers, is needed so that temporal patterns can be clearly traced and local practices within the Viking tradition of shipbuilding identified.

Arne Emil Christensen (1979) has summarised the present state of knowledge of sails and rigging from the few remains and from 7th to 12th century representations:

Standing rigging – shrouds, forestay and a backstay, which may have doubled as a halyard.

Running rigging – braces, sheets, tacks, a bowline to the leading edge of the sail supplemented by a *bietass* spar.

Sails – a loose-footed sail, possibly of wool, rectangular in shape with a low aspect ratio of $c\,0.6$.

We can recognise the seagoing abilities of the Viking Age cargo ship (albeit, structurally an open boat) in the fairly regular contact maintained between Iceland, Greenland and Scandinavia and in the countless voyages in the Baltic, the North Sea and eastern Atlantic and the Mediterranean. It might be expected that recent experimental work with replicas would tell us more about their performance: unfortunately much of this is poorly documented (McGrail, 1977). However, the relatively deep keels and the characteristic steepness of the lower strakes imply that Viking hulls had relatively good windward capability, and the use of the *bietass* to hold the leading edge of the sail taut shows that Viking seamen were striving to get close to the wind. Theoretical calculations indicate from the low value of the volumetric coefficient that the hull of the Gokstad ship had high speed potential (McGrail and Corlett, 1977); this is borne out to a degree by the relatively high speeds obtained during the National Maritime Museum's trial of a replica of the Gokstad *faering* (McGrail and McKee, 1974), when the craft may have been 'semi-planing'. The value of the Sail Area coefficient for the Gokstad ship indicates a good match between sail area and hull (Gillmer, 1979). Thus with a potentially fast hull and a well-matched sail, Viking seamanship could have obtained high sailing speeds in favourable conditions.

The light, buoyant structure of Viking ships meant that they could be used in relatively shallow water and up rivers, well inland. It is generally considered that, at least until the 11th century, they did not need the formal facilities of quays and jetties to load and unload. On suitable sites ships could be run aground, possibly onto simple hardstandings of parallel timbers on muddy beaches. Elsewhere ships could be anchored off a landing place or moored to posts in shallow water (scenes illustrated on the Bayeux Tapestry) to be loaded and unloaded by wading men or into carts or small boats.

Crumlin-Pedersen (1969, 24–7) has defined the differences between the mainstream of Viking shipbuilding and the Eastern Baltic or Slav variant. The latter had:

1 A 'keel' of T cross-section, but broader than deep;

2 A mast stepped in a transverse floor timber or in a step alongside a floor timber, rather than in a longitudinal keelson; and

3 Clinker planking fastened by treenails rather than clenched nails, with moss rather than hair or wool inserted in the overlap.

Ellmers (1972) has described 12 finds from east of the River Oder, none of them dated precisely and many of them lacking detailed records. Six of them had the mast stepped in a transverse timber – thus (although findspot is not necessarily place of origin) on present evidence a mast step in a transverse timber with other features being in the Viking tradition identifies the find as a 'Slavonic variant'. Other characteristics proposed as diagnostic are not so invariate. As noted by Crumlin-Pedersen (1969), three wrecks found east of the River Vistula (Baumgarth, Frevenburg 1 and 2) were clenched with iron nails with hair in the overlap, although they had masts in transverse timbers and keels that were broader than deep. Two boats from Ralswick (one with a mast step in a transverse timber) combine treenail fastenings and iron nails at stem and stern (boat 2) with hair in the overlap. Such variations might be expected in a large sample and need not affect the identification of a group, providing other characteristics are held in common: in this small sample such variability indicates that further evidence is required before the group can be defined.

Fastening planking by treenail or using moss in the overlaps cannot by themselves be diagnostic features as they have been found on medieval wrecks in Scandinavia and in the Netherlands which have other, non-Slavonic features. However, if they can be used in conjunction with other features, in particular the precise ratio of depth to breadth of keel, they may help to identify a distinctive Slavonic variant within the Viking tradition.

Southern Britain Apart from the possibly a-typical Graveney boat, there are no substantial, well-documented planked boat finds in Britain between the Sutton Hoo/Snape boats of the late 6th/early 7th centuries and the Kentmere extended logboat of *c* AD 1300. In post-Viking times, however, illustrations on the Bayeux Tapestry, on Irish monuments and on English, Irish and French town seals show a form of ship evidently in the Viking tradition; and the fragmented remains from the early 13th century site at Wood Quay, Dublin, have some of these features also. It is difficult to assess whether the features of the English post-Viking ship were solely due to the impact the Vikings had or whether there was a continuity of indigenous development from the East Anglian proto-Viking style of building which then merged with the main Viking tradition in the 10th and 11th centuries. In addition aspects of the Romano–Celtic tradition (as in Blackfriars 1) may have persisted in use. The Frisian tradition may also have influenced the English style of building for there are indications in Early English literature of the prominent part played by Frisians in Anglo-Saxon maritime affairs (Stenton, 1967, 219; Gordon, 1949, 343; Stevenson, 1959, 60). The ships which Alfred had built in AD 897 may thus have been influenced by proto-Viking, Romano–Celtic, Frisian and Viking traditions, despite the Chronicler's claim that they were 'neither after the Frisian design nor the Danish'.

The Graveney boat (Plate 21) of the early 10th century does indeed have features which may indicate mixed heredity. This boat, excavated in 1970 from a former tributary of the Thames (Fenwick,

1978), was originally about 14m long with a beam of c 3.9m. The relatively full midships body with broad beam, the heavy, closely-spaced floor timbers and the apparent absence of fixed crossbeams indicate that she was designed to carry a heavy cargo such as stone. She thus had a specialised function and her form and aspects of her structure may therefore be unrepresentative of 10th century Anglo-Saxon boatbuilding.

Her shell build with planking clenched by iron nails with hair in the overlap, the floor timbers fastened by treenails, and the use of stringers are in the Viking tradition: but the form of the sternpost with its pronounced heel, the hooked hood-ends of the planking where they are fastened to the sternpost, and the method of driving the plank-fastening iron nails through a treenail are not. Fenwick (1978, 224) has drawn attention to the use of nails driven through treenails in the timbers of cargo ships of the Classical Mediterranean and of Blackfriars 1 boat. The Bruges boat fragments, recently dated to c AD 180 ± 80 (Har-472), and now thought to be of the Romano-Celtic tradition, also had nails driven though birch treenails in a transverse floor timber. The pronounced heel on Graveney's raking sternpost may be functional but it has parallels (not in conjunction with a raking sternpost) on some Dorestad Carolingian coins (see Ellmers, 1972, 56, fig.39e-h). Angular heels are also seen on ships on 9th century Hedeby coins and on other 7th to 9th century Scandinavian representations (Fenwick, 1978, 215-16), which Crumlin-Pedersen (1965) attributes to influence from the Frisian/Lower Rhine area. Thus there are suggestions in the Graveney boat of influences from Frisian, Romano-Celtic and Viking traditions.

Fenwick (1978, 251) argues that the ship on the 13th century seal of Faversham with raking stems, and those on Faversham and Winchelsea seals of the 14th century with raking stems and prominent treenail heads at the frame stations, continue some of the Graveney features. She also sees continuity in the hooked, hood-ends illustrated in a 13th century English manuscript (1978, 233, fig.8.25). Furthermore Crumlin-Pedersen has drawn attention to parallels between the Graveney boat and the sternpost and plank ends of the 15th century Blackfriars 3 ship (Marsden, 1971, Plate 5). But these are isolated, and any generalisation about a continuing tradition must await more evidence.

Later ships in the Viking tradition The evidence for the 'post-classic' phase of Viking shipbuilding is

Plate 21   The Graveney boat during excavation in 1970. Photo NMM.

almost entirely representational. Murals in the 13th century church at Sikjon, Telemark, Norway, and the 14th century one at Skamstrup, Zealand, Denmark, show the use of stern rudders and battle platforms. On 13th and 14th century town seals from Ireland, England and France, we can see complex rigging and the use of reef points and bowsprits, the addition of castles forward and aft, crossbeams protruding through the sides, and the introduction of a mast crutch or 'myke', now also known from the Wood Quay excavations. The English word for a Scandi-navian style of ship appears to have been *ceol* or 'keel'; and the word is also used in contexts which probably refer to English ships built in this tradition (McCusker, 1966, 288–9). A future investigation of a wreck in the River Hamble, Hampshire, thought to be that of the early 15th century *Grace Dieu*, may reveal more about the final stages of this form of shipbuilding.

The Viking ship in her 'post-classic' form appears to have been replaced as the dominant ship in Northern waters from the 12th century, but aspects of this building tradition lived on in the small boats of West Norway and Shetland until the 20th century.

The cog The link between the documented medi-eval ship type name 'cog' and representations on 14th century seals (Plate 22) was established by Fliedner (1964; 1972, 23), and Crumlin-Pedersen (1965) used this and other evidence to demonstrate that early ships of this tradition had the following characteristics:
Flat, keel-less (or keel plank) bottom with flush-laid planking;
Distinctive sharp transition between bottom and inclined stems;
Steep clinker-built sides; and
One square-rigged mast.
Crumlin-Pedersen has argued for a Frisian/lower

Rhine origin for this tradition, and following Vogel he equates Alfred's 'Frisian design' with the cog of the 9th century, a time when this type-name was first associated in documents with Frisian shipping and trade (Jellema, 1955, 32).

The early cog was probably an open boat, but by the 9th century, when Anskar took passage in a Frisian vessel with two cabins (Robinson, 1921, 43), the cog may have become a ship. Ellmers (1979) has traced other structural changes in the cog from a study of 13th and 14th century town seals (Plate 22). Around AD 1242 the stern rudder replaced a T-handled, tiller-less rudder which had been raised or lowered on the lee side to alter course. Early 13th century side planking overlapped the stemposts but by c 1280 this joint was protected by a false stem. Later cogs had more superstructure than early ones.

From an examination of the Bremen cog wreck recovered from the River Weser between 1962 and 1965, Ellmers (1979) has added six further features to those enumerated by Crumlin-Pedersen:
(a) a keel plank
(b) side planking fastened by iron nails clenched by turning the point back into the timber
(c) moss in the seams, kept in place by laths and iron butterfly-shaped clamps
(d) mast step in keelson
(e) knee-shaped 'bulkheads'
(f) protruding crossbeams
These characteristics may apply only to ships late in this tradition, for the Bremen cog has been dated by dendrochronology to c AD 1380 (Fliedner, 1972, 34). She is c 23.50m × 7.50m × 5.30m, and Ellmers has deduced she was built in the following sequence:
1 Keel-plank scarfed to stems. Four bottom planks laid out flush and flat over the midship section but turned to fit into the stem rabbets.
2 Bottom planking treenailed to 40 floor timbers.
3 A flush strake set at an angle to the bottom, form-

ing the turn of the bilge each side—these appear to be fastened to the floor timbers.

4   Four clinker strakes fitted each side, using the characteristically turned nails. After clenching, outer top edge of lower plank cut away, moss inserted and held by lath and clamps. The strakes overlap the stems to which they are spiked.

5   Futtocks (lower-side frames) scarfed to floor timbers, joggled to fit the overlaps and treenailed to planking.

6   Five crossbeams fitted, four protruding through the ship's sides on top of 4th side strake.

7   Four more strakes fitted each side in a similar manner to the lower ones. False stem fitted.

8   Upper side frames support these upper strakes; four knee-shaped 'bulkheads' fitted on top of cross-beams.

9   Ceiling planking fitted as far as the 4th side strake; keelson with mast step notched to fit over 22 floor timbers.

10   Longitudinal (carling) timbers, let into the top surface of 'bulkheads' to support decking approximately level with top of 6th side strake.

11   Stern platform fitted.

Other finds identified as cogs include: Danzig Brosen, Poland; Kalmar 5, Sweden; Wreck Q75, Netherlands (Ellmers, 1972) and Kolding, Vejby and Kollerup from Denmark (Crumlin-Pedersen, 1979): they range in date from 13th century to c AD 1500. All have a sharp transition between bottom and stems; and all have a keel plank in a flat, flush-laid bottom with clinker laid sides, with the exception of Kalmar 5, which has clinker bottom planking, and possibly Q75 where the details of the side planking and the bottom/stems transition are not available. Other cog characteristics (as defined above) are not so well represented, in particular clenching nails by turning has been noted only in Kalmar 5, and moss-with-lath caulking and metal clamps is reported only on the Vejby find. Protruding crossbeams were found on the Kolding wreck and Kalmar 5; bulk-heads in Kalmar 5 and Kollerup; and a mast step in a keelson in Kolding and Vejby, but in a transverse timber in the Kollerup wreck. Reinders (1979) has described three finds from the Dutch polders dated stratigraphically to the early 14th century, with clinker laid sides and ends, and a flush-laid bottom. All have moss in the seams with a lath held in place by iron clamps or treenails. Reinders prudently refrains from calling them 'cogs'.

When the full range of data is available for all these finds it should be possible to recognise more clearly the characteristic features of a cog and to identify variations due to changes with time, regional building techniques, and possibly differing functions and operating conditions.

Waterproofing seams by inserting organic material topped by a longitudinal lath which is then held in position by a sewn, wooden or metal fastening is found in several parts of the world. In Europe it is

Plate 22   The AD 1329 seal of Stralsund, depicting a cog. Photo: NMM.

known from the Bronze Age Ferriby and Brigg boats and a similar but not identical technique is found in the Romano–Celtic barges Yverdon and Bevaix (although the planking is flushlaid rather than clinker), and it persisted for many centuries in the lower Rhine region. Another distinctive cog feature, clenching a nail by turning, is also found in the Romano–Celtic tradition although here it is used to fasten planking to floor and side timbers rather than to clench-fasten planking. When these points are considered in conjunction with the theory of the pre-9th century origin of the cog in the Frisian/Lower Rhine region, they emphasise the importance of the Romano–Celtic tradition to any study of early medieval building techniques.

Documentary evidence indicates that the cog became dominant in northern seas during the late 12th/early 13th centuries when the Hanseatic merchants (and the Teutonic knights) required a ship with great cargo capacity. Opinions are divided as to why the cog was developed in size rather than the ship of Viking tradition. However, a flat-bottomed, wall-sided cog could carry relatively more cargo than the round-hulled Viking form, and, as Basil Greenhill (1976, 259) has pointed out, a flat-bottomed design requires less skill and is therefore cheaper to build. The 14th century Bremen cog and the three 13th/14th century Danish finds had sawn planking (personal communication; Ellmers and Crumlin-Pedersen): cog builders may therefore have adopted at an early date this type of planking, which is more economic to produce, albeit less strong, than the split planking of the Viking ship. Operationally, the cog had the advantage that she could take the ground easily and sit upright as the tide ebbed. Further research is required, but it may also be that the cog's vertical-motion rudder was superior to the side rudder, and the cog structure more easily adapted to the even more effective stern rudder; and cog seamen may have been readier than Viking ship seamen to forgo auxiliary propulsion by oar thus allowing high unobstructed sides, which increased capacity and deterred pirates. Whatever the reasons, the cog not only came to prominence in northern Europe but subsequently influenced Mediterranean shipbuilding.

The hulc   The hulc, another documented medieval type with a probable Low Countries origin, appears to have become the dominant type in the 14th century, although in the early 15th century the same ship could evidently be called a cog or a hulc (McCusker, 1966, 284–5). The inscription on the *c* AD 1295 town seal of New Shoreham, Sussex, links the depicted ship with the former name of the town, Hulkesmouth. The word 'hulc', first mentioned in the late 10th/early 11th century laws of Aethelred 2 (Robertson, 1925, 71), probably means something hollowed like a peapod, and the ship depicted on the Shoreham seal has a banana shape in outline. Furthermore, the planking appears to run in a uniform curve parallel to sheerline and bottom, ending on a horizontal line at the ends, well above the waterline. Similar characteristics may be seen on the Winchester (Plate 23) and Zedelgem, Bruges, fonts of *c* 1180, the 14th century coins found in the Vejby wreck (Crumlin-Pedersen, 1979, 25), the late 15th century coins excavated from the Royal Naval College, Greenwich (Greenhill, 1976, 284), and possibly on some Carolingian coins from Dorestad (Ellmers, 1972, fig.39 a–d). On the latter, a side rudder appears to be in use and possibly oars as well as a sail. An engraving on a 7th century Merovingian strap end from northern France (Joffroy, 1978) may also be of this general type.

Crumlin-Pedersen (1965) believes that the boat found in Utrecht (boat 1) in 1930 incorporates these characteristics. A radiocarbon date of 790 ± AD 50 has been published, and although the discussion of this (Philipsen, 1965, 37) is inconclusive, a date in the second half of the 1st millennium AD is probably warranted. This boat has an oak logboat base, curved longitudinally and transversely, and extended at the ends by planking. Three overlapping washstrakes with moss caulking are treenailed on each side. The centre washstrakes are half-logs with curved side outboard: thus the top strake is 'reverse-clinker'. At the ends the planking is fastened by iron nails to small transoms. Thirty-eight naturally curved floor timbers, alternately long and short, are fastened to the planking; at the ends of the boat they were probably topped by crossbeams with knees to the sides. There is a small (towing) mast step set in a floor timber about one third the way from the bow.

If this is indeed an early form of hulc then the characteristics of this tradition are:

longitudinal and transverse curve of hull;
no visible stems or keel; and
clinker planking which terminates in a transom (early) or on a horizontal line (late).

One of the three boats found in 1974 at Utrecht (boat III = 4) is similar to the 1930 boat and is dated stratigraphically to the late 12th century (Hoekstra, 1975). Ellmers (1972, fig.35) has argued that one of the 11th century boats found at Antwerp in 1905 was also a hulc: it was similar in form to Utrecht 1 but

from the diagram published by Ellmers the flush-laid washstrakes seem to end neither on a horizontal line nor in a transom and thus this find lacks one of the supposed main hulc attributes. Marsden (1976, 49) wishes to classify Zwammerdam boat 3 (de Weerd, 1978) with Utrecht 1, but the former seems to be a logboat extended by one strake without any of the hulc characteristics.

If we may judge from harbour dues and taxation laws, the hulc and the *ceol* (probably the English equivalent of a Viking tradition cargo ship) were about the same size at the end of the 10th century; in the early 12th century the *ceol* was bigger than the hulc; but by the 14th century the hulc was bigger than the *ceol* (McCusker, 1966, 279–80). The indications may be, therefore, that the hulc dominated northern sea commerce in the 14th century because she had been developed to have greater capacity: this may be an early example of taxation influencing ship design. There may also have been technological reasons for this dominance—for example, if we may judge by the Zedelgem font, the hulc early adopted the stern rudder. However, at present, the hulc tradition is ill-defined, and will remain so until a 14th century example is excavated, although further research into the Romano–Celtic tradition and the early medieval boats of the Low Countries may

Plate 23   Scenes from the life of St Nicholas on the late 12th century font in Winchester Cathedral. The ship is believed to represent a hulc. Photo: NMM.

39

throw light on its origins.

Within 100 years or so of its heyday, the hulc appears to have been replaced by the skeleton-built, non-edge-joined ship. However, as we know nothing about the internal structure of the 14th century hulc we should not discount the theoretical possibility that some were skeleton-built.

The Punt   Ellmers (1972) has argued that certain medieval finds known as *praams*, ferries or punts may form a distinctive boatbuilding tradition, and Crumlin-Pedersen (1978) links these boats to the Rhine 'barges' of the Romano–Celtic tradition. The 20 or so finds thought to be of this form (Vreta Gård, Haithabu, Egernsund (Plate 24), Utrecht 2 ($=$ 1), Antwerp 1 to 4, Falsterbo 1 to 6, Elbing, Ellerwald, Novgorod (several) and Treiden) date from the 7th to the 15th centuries (Ellmers, 1972). Their common characteristics are a flattish, flush-laid, keel-less bottom, and a sharp transition between bottom and sides generally formed by an L-shaped transition strake sometimes associated with L-shaped floor timbers: these features are also found in the Romano–Celtic group. Where they can be measured, the L/B ratio $\simeq$ 5 and the L/D ratio $\simeq$ 17; both values being slightly less than those for the Romano–Celtic 'barges'. Other features are either not recorded or

they are too varied for them to be thought of as group characteristics. It remains to be demonstrated that this is a definable tradition.

Sail in northern Europe   The use of sails by the early medieval Irish and Picts was chronicled by Gildas, a British monk writing in the early 6th century, and by Adomnan of mid-6th century Iona. Procopius claimed that the 6th century inhabitants of Britain did not have sail. However, Claudian, Sidonius Apollinaris and Gildas imply that the Saxons of the 4th and 5th centuries did, and it may be that Procopius was referring to war craft rather than to cargo carriers. By the early 8th century references to sail by Bede and other English authors take the matter beyond doubt. An engraving on a strap end from northern France (Joffrey, 1978) depicting a mast with rigging, suggests that sail was used in France from at least the early 7th century, and indeed there may be continuity from earlier use (p.25). The earliest evidence for sail in Scandinavia are the 6th century AD ship figures of type B on the Gotland Stones (Marstrander, 1976, 21). The Scandinavian word for sail, *sigla*, appears to be a borrowing from Frisian (Jellima, 1955, 27) and it is thus possible that sail was introduced to the Baltic by early Frisian traders. Although the sprit and lateen were known in the

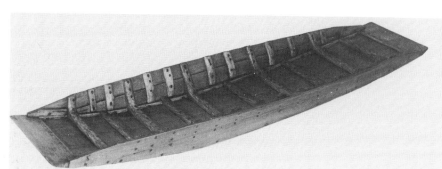

Plate 24   A 1:10 model of the 11th century AD Egernsund boat excavated by Ole Crumlin-Pedersen.
Photo: Ole Crumlin-Pedersen.

Classical Mediterranean (see below), the evidence in northern Europe appears to point only to the square sail from earliest times until almost the end of the medieval period.

Southern planked craft

At the end of the Roman period in the West, Byzantium used vessels similar in form to those of Classical times, the 'round' merchant sailing ships and the 'long' galleys propelled by oar and sail: a division of roles paralleled in the Viking tradition. The lateen and the spritsail, as well as the square sail, were already in use in the Mediterranean by this time. The square sail was generally on a single mast, but foremasts are known from the 6th century BC (Casson, 1980), and in their *artemon* forward-raked form, from the 1st century AD (Casson, 1971, 240). Ships with a third, mizzen, mast are known from the 3rd century BC (Casson, 1971, 197). The sprit was in use from at least the 2nd century BC; the 'Arab' lateen (that is a 'settee' with a short luff) from the 2nd century AD, and the triangular form from the 4th century AD (Casson, 1971, 244).

Three excavated craft contribute to our knowledge of medieval shipping in this region. A 4th century AD wreck off Yassi Ada, Turkey, excavated between 1958 and 1974, was a small merchantman generally in the Graeco-Roman tradition, including the shell building sequence (van Doorninck, 1976). However, some iron fastenings were used, and the draw-tongued joint plank fastenings were spaced at *c* 250 mm, much wider than in earlier ships. In addition, the tenons in these joints were tapered, thus making it simpler for planks to be fitted together. The second Yassi Ada wreck, dated by associated coins to the 7th century AD, was a double-ended cargo ship. A through beam near amidships supported the mast, and two through beams near the stern are thought to be part of a mounting for two side steering oars, probably as depicted on the 6th century AD mosaic in Sant' Apollinare Nuovo, Ravenna (Bass, 1972, 54). The plank fastenings were 300–400 mm apart at the stern and up to 900 mm elsewhere (Casson, 1971, 208–9), and the tenons were not held in position by treenails. The framing was more massive than in the earlier ship and was fastened to the planking by iron fastenings rather than treenails. Thus the ship shows more reliance on her internal framework and less on the planking. The sequence of building seems to confirm this relative importance: up to the waterline, building followed the shell sequence with 16 strakes being edge-joined; at this point frames were inserted and wales and upper planking were fastened to them. These upper strakes were not edge-joined, and thus the upper hull was built in skeleton sequence with the shape being determined by the upper frames. This change in techniques is also seen in the Pantano Longarini wreck found in Sicily in 1964 (Bass, 1972) and dated *c* AD 622 ± 48 (P–1435). The same sequence as in the contemporary Yassi Ada ship was used, and the fastenings in the lower planking were even further apart, averaging 990 mm.

Documentary sources mention types of vessel by name but, as in northern Europe, there are difficulties in giving precise characteristics to them. However, with due caution, some of the iconographic and documentary evidence may be considered:

DROMON   The Byzantine warship of the 5th to 10th centuries AD was a light, swift ship with one or two tiers of oars worked through oarports on the larger ships or on an outrigger on the smaller ones (Casson, 1971, 151). These were probably lateen rigged as shown in a late 9th century Greek manuscript now in the Bibliothèque Nationale (Villain-Gandossi, 1979, 197, fig.12.1).

GALLEY   By the 14th century Genoa and Venice had

merchant galleys similar in form to the dromon but with two or even three lateen rigged masts, and two side steering oars. Every bench had two oarsmen on both sides, each working an oar; subsequently a third oarsman and oar were added. These galleys were used in the North Sea as well as the Mediterranean, and Venice maintained a galley service to Flanders and England from 1313 to 1533.

NEF   In the 12th and 13th centuries 'nef' appears to refer to a specific type: a dumpy, high-sided ship with two or three decks and fore and after 'castles', the upper part of which were fighting tops. Generally these ships had two lateen rigged masts and side steering oars.

COG AND CARRACK   The Florentine chronicler Giovanni Villani recorded that in 1304 Bayonnese pirates brought cogs into the Mediterranean. Their combination of axial rudder with square sail on a single mast evidently gave them better handling qualities than the contemporary large Mediterranean vessels, and so these features were adopted, the first *cocha* being mentioned at Genoa in 1311. Subsequently a lateen rigged mizzen was added to the square main, and then a small square-rigged foremast. At about this time the term *carrack* began to be used, but the characteristics of this mid-14th century vessel are not yet known (van der Merwe, personal communication).

Shells, skeletons and edge-joined planking

As Basil Greenhill (1976, 289) has emphasised, the late 15th century three-masted, non-edge-joined, skeleton-built ship became the means by which Europeans 'discovered' all the seas of the world. Where and when this combination of features originated is not at present clear. Three masts had been early known in the Mediterranean and they were used there in the 14th century. The idea of using a skeleton or framework to give the form of a boat had been familiar to skinboat builders from prehistoric times. Extending a logboat may also involve inserting a framework of ribs before the washstrakes are added (McGrail, 1978), although this has not so far been reported on an excavated boat. Repairs to a planked vessel would also familiarise shipbuilders with additions to an existing framework. Medieval church builders were familiar with the erection of frameworks and the use of moulds to produce a predetermined shape.

Thus the general concept of skeleton building was available in many regions of Europe to be applied to shipbuilding. In northern Europe the bottom planking of the cog, and the earlier, Romano–Celtic barges, was not edge-joined but fastened to the floor timbers. Shape was thus at least partly determined by framework and the hull made watertight by added caulking. For the Mediterranean, Morrison (1976, 165–6) has pointed out that a form of skeleton building may have been known in the 5th century BC. Tchiernia (1978) has noted that, although all planking was edge-fastened, the 1st century BC wreck Madrague de Giens was built in a mixture of shell and skeleton sequence, with the form of the hull between the 4th and 13th strakes being determined by the shape of the floor timbers. The 7th century AD wrecks from Yassi Ada and Pantano Longarini had edge-joined and non-edge-joined planking, and shell and skeleton sequences. In all three ships the skeleton sequence appears to have been used where minimum fashioning of the planking would have been required. Nevertheless, part-skeleton techniques *were* used: did this become full skeleton build at an early date? There are three cases, albeit poorly documented, of possible skeleton build in the 11th–12th century Mediterranean:

1 Casson (1971, 203) states that an 11th century boat from the Po valley was skeleton built.

2 A wreck of the early 11th century from Serçe

Liman, Turkey, is reported to be skeleton built (Bass, 1978, 790).

3 A 12th century wreck in the Northern Sporades, Greece may have no edge-joining (Bass, 1972, 146). In addition, it is not impossible that some 14th century hulcs and contemporary Mediterranean ships were skeleton built. However, the evidence available at present is insufficient to support an hypothesis that skeleton building was the norm in either northern or southern Europe before the 14th century.

Several reasons may be advanced to explain why this change to skeleton building took place, whether it was a gradual process or revolutionary. The choice of shell or skeleton sequence generally determines three things:

(a) how the required shape is obtained:

SHELL SEQUENCE   By inherited wisdom and indoctrination; by eye, possibly with temporary moulds or a few measurements and comparisons (see p.32).

SKELETON SEQUENCE   By active frames (permanent moulds) constructed to a pre-determined shape (a design).

(b) where the structural strength lies:

SHELL SEQUENCE   The edge-joined planking generally found with this sequence makes the hull, keel and stems a continuous load-bearing structure; the inserted frames or ribs reinforce this.

SKELETON SEQUENCE   With the non-edge-joined planking generally found with this sequence, the framework of stems, keel and frames becomes the principal loadbearing structure. Caulking then puts some compression into the planking.

(c) how the hull is made watertight:

SHELL SEQUENCE   Planking is close fitting (Classical) or overlapped (Scandinavian). Organic material and tar fill irregularities.

SKELETON SEQUENCE   By inserted caulking material (which also enables the hull to cope with limited shear loads).

The advantages and disadvantages of the two methods are:

1 It seems likely that there is a practical limit to the length of an edge-joined, shell structure, beyond which shearing forces cannot be absorbed. On the other hand by using suitably stout timber for the framework, a skeleton-built ship can be extended to great size.

2 In the skeleton sequence a special skill is required to design the active frames; once these are made, less skill is needed to build the hull. On the other hand special supervisory skill is necessary throughout the shaping of a shell-built, edge-joined hull, although 'rules of thumb' and planking aids may help. Patterns of active frames can be used many times independently of the initial skill in making them and in addition it seems likely that when patterns are available, a skeleton hull can be built more quickly than a shell hull.

3 Planking can be repaired more readily in skeleton build, which is therefore more economic.

4 Better quality timber is required for shell building as the planking is more highly stressed. Radially split oak planking, which gives greatest strength for thickness, was generally used in northern medieval shell-built vessels until at least the 12th century (McGrail, 1974, 42–4). Sawn boards, a more economical way of converting logs, came into shipbuilding use from the 14th century, or earlier. Whilst not so strong as split planking, it was entirely adequate for skeleton build and could be of the thickness necessary to retain caulking.

Thus, by skeleton building, a bigger and longer ship could be given sufficient strength and stiffness to remain acceptably watertight; such a structure would also accept gun ports through the sides. There were also economies of scale, and timber of not such high quality (including sawn boards) could be used.

Arabia

Technologically the Neolithic inhabitants of this region were capable of making any of the basic types of raft or boat. In Mesopotamia the Rivers Tigris and Euphrates gave access to the raw material of the highlands to the north; the Persian Gulf was the gateway to international trade: thus water transport was an essential aspect of the civilisation that developed here (back endpaper). Reed was abundant and probably used for houses as well as boats; by *c* 4000 BC the technique of waterproofing reeds with bitumen had evidently been acquired (Clark and Piggott, 1976, 180).

Non-planked craft

Reed rafts and boats   A pictogram on a clay tablet of the 4th millennium BC has a double-ended vessel with high curving ends and vertical lines across the hull, which suggest a reed bundle raft of boat shape (Bass, 1972, 12; fig.1). Engravings on cylinder seals dated to the end of this millennium show similarly shaped craft in outline (Bass, 1972, figs.8 and 9): their ends appear to be bent over and tied inboard leading to the belief that they also represent reed craft. An engraving on a later seal of *c* 2300 BC (Casson, 1971, fig.21) has the vertical 'binding' lines and a side steering oar. The almost vertical ends of this craft are a distinctive feature on models and other representations from this region. Similar ends can also be seen on rock carvings and pottery of 4th millennium Egypt, sometimes on craft which are apparently differentiated as 'foreign' (Bass, 1972, 12–13, 27). A craft of this form with a pole mast and

rectangular sail (Plate 25) on an Egyptian late Gerzean vase dated to *c* 3100 BC is the earliest evidence for sail anywhere (but see the Eridu model on p.45). Assyrian documents of *c* 2000 BC record that reed was used for watercraft (Casson, 1971, 6), and rafts of reed are still in use today in the Persian Gulf region.

Representations from the area to the north of the Persian Gulf which do not have the 'binding' lines may depict reed boats waterproofed with bitumen, rather than reed rafts. The earliest reference to boats of this type is in an inscription dated *c* 2300 BC in which Sargon of Akkad claims to have been placed in the river as a baby in a basket of rushes sealed with bitumen (Anderson, 1978, 49). A comparable story

Plate 25   Craft with rectangular sail on a vase from Naqada, Egypt dated to *c* 3100 BC. Drawing after Bass, 1972, 13.

is told about Moses (*Exodus*, 2, 3). Strabo (16.1.15) described similar boats in Babylonia in the 1st century AD, whether round or elongated was not stated. In the mid-19th century, Layard (1853, 552) noted small, boat-shaped craft in the marshes of southern Iraq with 'a narrow framework of rushes covered with bitumen', known as *taradas* or 'black boats'. The modern *tarada* (Thesiger, 1978, figs.9 and 15) has a profile with high ends similar to that on the early representations described above but is planked. However, Thesiger (1978, 128, fig.45) describes a boat-shaped craft, the *zaima* (Plate 5), made of reed bundles with an inserted stiffening of light willows and coated externally with bitumen: this seems similar to the river *jillabie* described by Heyerdahl (1978, 35). The modern *quffa* (cognate with Akkadian *quppa*) is a circular boat also made of reed bundles ('coiled basketry') covered with bitumen (Plate 26), and was first noted on the River Euphrates in the late 17th century (Hornell, 1970, 104–5). It may be that this is the type depicted on the 9th century BC reliefs of

Ashur-nasir-pal which appears to have a smooth skin rather than the patchwork of hides seen on later reliefs.

It thus seems possible that two types of reed boat, one round, one elongated, were in use in the prehistoric period, as well as boat-shaped reed rafts.

Buoyed rafts The use of wooden rafts buoyed by skin floats and propelled by oars is shown on Assyrian reliefs of the 7th century BC from the Palace of Sennacherib (Fig.1 in Casson, 1971) where they carry blocks of stone. Xenophon (*Anabasis* 2.4.28) mentions the use of 'leather rafts' on the Tigris in the 5th century BC, and indeed buoyed rafts, known as *kelek*, supported by hundreds of goat skins (Plate 26), were used in the 20th century to bring goods from Kurdistan to Baghdad (Hornell, 1970, 106). Pliny (*H.N.* 6.35) writing in c AD 77 describes their use in the Gulf of Aden, and a 1st/2nd century AD guide to the Indian Ocean, *Periplus of the Erythraean Sea*, Ch.27 (Huntingford, 1980), describes similar rafts which carried frankincense to Kane, thought to be Hisn Ghurab near Bir Ali, c 240 m east of Aden. They may well have been used in other coastal waters.

Skin boats A clay model dated c 3400 BC from a grave at Eridu in southern Mesopotamia is almost elliptical in plan and has a vertical socket in the base and three holes through the sides near the top edge (Casson, 1971, fig.20). Bass (1972, 12) believes this may represent a skin boat with fittings for a mast, but Casson (1971, 22) thinks that the socket may be for a ceremonial staff and the other holes for suspension. Other evidence for skin boats comes from 2nd millennium BC Assyrian documents (Casson, 1971, 6; Bass, 1972, 14), which include hide in the boat-building materials they list, and Assyrian reliefs of the 7th century BC, which show boats of apparently rounded form carrying building material. The sides

Plate 26 A 20th century buoyed raft (*kelek*) and reed boats (*quffa*) on the River Tigris. Photo: Hornell, 1970 plate IVB.

of these boats are marked into small rectangular areas generally thought to be hides sewn together (Plate 27). In these reliefs two men are depicted sitting on benches at the ends of the boat pulling oars in opposite directions – it is probable that one pair should be shown pushing rather than pulling. Herodotus (1.194), who visited Babylon in the 5th century BC, described round boats of hide stretched over a willow frame (although he evidently confused their use with that of the *kelek*) and Strabo (16.4.19) noted the use of skin boats to cross the Red Sea in the 1st century AD. Hornell (1970, 104) described early 19th century 'circular boats of basketwork covered with skins' in use near Baghdad. If this basketwork was woven as seems likely, rather than coiled basketry, these craft are properly classified as skin boats, possibly among

Plate 27   A 7th century BC Assyrian relief from Sennacherib's palace at Nineveh – possibly representing a skin boat. BM 124822. Photo: Trustees of the British Museum.

the last to be used in this region, as they are unknown today.

Logboats and log rafts   Ammianus (24.4.8) noted that logboats (*monoxylon*) were used on the Euphrates in the 4th century AD. Abundant reed and an increasing shortage of suitable trees (Johnstone, 1980, 182) may have meant that logboats did not become a widespread form of water transport in this region. Log rafts are not known until mid-19th century travellers' reports (Bowen, 1952, 192–3), and these are small simple ones of two or three logs lashed together.

Planked craft

Sumerian, Akkadian and Assyrian texts written on clay tablets in the period *c* 2500 BC to *c* 500 BC indicate that planked boats were in use on the Tigris and Euphrates (Bass, 1972, 18). Casson (1971, 23–8) has deduced that these boats were built on a keel plank in the shell sequence with the planking edge-joined by dovetail clamps and mortice and tenon joints (similar to the roughly contemporary Egyptian Dahshur boats) and with inserted ribs and crossbeams. The boats were coated inside with fish oil and outside with bitumen and were propelled by a cloth or reed sail and by oar: boats using the extensive canal systems could be paddled, punted or towed. Other possible evidence of planked boats comes from two seals excavated at or near Bahrein (Johnstone, 1980, 176, figs.13.8 and 13.9) and dated to the end of the 3rd millennium BC showing boats with a mast near amidships. One has slight and the other a marked sheer at the ends and the straight, slightly raked stems join the bottom line of the boat at a well-defined angle. Planked boats therefore seem to have been in use as well as reed craft in the 3rd millennium BC, and it is from this period we have records of voyages from Babylon through the Persian Gulf to

Telmun or Dilmun (?Bahrein); to Makkan or Magan (?Oman); and to Meluhha or Melukhkha (?Dhufar on the south coast of Arabia or an Harappan port of western India) (Casson, 1971, 23–4; Hourani, 1963, 6; Bowen, 1952, 192).

The Periplus (Chapter 36) mentions that at Ommana, on the Persian side of the Gulf of Oman, sewn plank boats known as *madarata* (= fastened with palm fibre) were built and exported to Hadramaut and Yemen. In other regions (north-west Europe–see Chapter 3; the Mediterranean–see Casson (1971, 9–10)) sewn planking appears to have preceded planking with wooden fastenings. By analogy, therefore, the sewing technique may have been in use in the Arabian area much earlier than the 1st century AD.

Procopius (*Bell. Pers* 1.19.23) writing in the 6th century AD mentions sewn boats in the Persian Gulf, and further references to them were made from the 10th century through to the 20th (Hornell, 1970, 234; Hourani, 1963, 92–7; Lane-Fox, 1875, 413). The 12th century chronicler ibn-Jubayr mentions the use of *dusur* in the building of sewn boats. Hourani (1963, 97–8) wishes to translate this as caulking; however, as he shows, it can also mean treenails which seems more likely as treenails were used on recent Arab boats to fasten the planking in conjunction with sewing (Bowen, 1956, 284–5, fig.3D). Apart from this and the fact that such a boat, including rigging and sails, could be made from the coconut tree alone (Hourani, 1963, 91) we learn little about constructional details from these medieval reports. A painting accompanying the AD 1237 Mesopotamian manuscript known as Al Hariri's Maqāmāt (Bib. Nat. Ms. arabe 5847 fol.119) shows a double-ended vessel with sewn planking (stitching paired with gaps) which seems to be flush-laid (Plate 28). The stems are high (the after one being almost vertical, the forward one more raked) and join the bottom at a marked angle.

She has a stern rudder although, as Johnstone (1980, 191) points out, a 14th century version of this drawing shows a side rudder. There are obvious points of resemblance with 20th century Arabian sewn boats as described by Hornell (1970, 235–6) and Bowen (1952). Although some of the traditional features of medieval Arab planked boatbuilding persisted in certain areas, the arrival of Portuguese ships at the end of the 15th century had a marked effect. Johnstone and Muir (1962, 59) conclude from a philological study that there was a change from shell to skeleton sequence, and iron nails, caulking, and a transom stern were introduced. However, fish oil continues to the present day to be applied to the upper planking, with a mixture of lime, fat and gum to the planking under water.

If the Eridu model is discounted, sailing is known in this region from c 2500–2000 BC (Casson, 1971, 23) with a sail of cloth or reed. The shape is unknown, but the sail on what may be an Arabian boat depicted on the c 3100 BC Gerzean vase from Egypt (Plate 25), is rectangular. Strabo (16.1.9) described sails made of reed in the 1st century AD. The 'Arab' lateen sail was known in the Mediterranean from at least the 2nd century AD (Casson, 1971, 244), but its origin as an Arabian sail is unproven. Hourani (1963, 103) sees possible references to a triangular sail in 9th and 10th century Arab literature, but this evidence is unsubstantial.

We have little indication of the detailed performance of early Arab craft, but from at least the 1st century AD they undertook direct ocean voyages to India, using the S.W. monsoon in July/October and the N.E. in November/March (*Periplus*, Chapters 39, 57, 60). An aspect of this trade which continued from early times to the present day was the import of timber from the Malabar coast of India (Hourani, 1963, 33). Timber was imported to Lagash, north of Ur in c 2450 BC (Johnstone, 1980, 182) and to the

Persian Gulf from north-west India in the 1st/2nd century AD (*Periplus*, Chapter 36). Hourani (1963, 90) believes that there is evidence for the import of Indian teak as early as *c* 300 BC to build ships at Tylus (Bahrein), however, the Arab word for mast, *diql* (= palm tree), indicates that some local timber was used in early times.

Timothy Severin has built a replica of a medieval Arab sewn boat (insofar as this is possible) and plans to sail from the Persian Gulf to China, a voyage which he believes lies behind some of the Sinbad stories, the earliest elements of which have been ascribed to the late 9th century AD. We may expect to learn something of early Arab seamanship from this experiment in due course.

Plate 28   Illustration of a sewn plank boat from al-Harīrī's *Maqāmāt* of AD 1237.
Photo: Bibliothèque Nationale, Paris.

Africa

Plate 29   Craft depicted on an Amratian bowl (top) and a rock carving from Wadi Hammamat, Egypt (bottom): both dated to the 4th millennium BC. Drawing after Bass, 1972. 13.

This continent encompasses many different ecologies and peoples but, although much is known about boat types in recent use, knowledge of early forms of water transport outside Egypt is limited. Except for skin and the rare bark raft and reed boat, all basic watercraft types are or have been present in the Continent. However, bark boats are only known in and around Rhodesia.

Non-planked craft

Reed craft   Graffitti and paintings on pots and other artifacts of 4th millennium BC Egypt appear to show two types of craft: one with high, almost vertical ends (Bass, 1972, 13, fig.3), similar to representations found in Mesopotamia (p.44); and another with a more curved but low profile which later became sickle-shaped (Plate 29). These craft generally have a structure amidships, a single steering oar and are propelled by paddle or possibly by oar. On rock carvings from Wadi Hammamat dated to the late 4th millennium, such boats have vertical 'reed binding' lines, and indeed nothing in this millennium can unambiguously be identified as representing a planked boat. A linen fragment from Heirakonpolis (Bass, 1972, 27, fig.7) shows steersman and crew facing forward and so it might be thought that these were paddled craft, but modern methods of rowing are known which would be consistent with this illustration (McGrail and Farrell, 1979). A Mesopotamian-style craft on a late Gerzean pot dated to *c* 3100 BC with a pole mast and rectangular sail stepped near one end (Plate 25) is the first evidence

for sail. However, what appears to be a palm branch in the bows of earlier representations may be for propulsion as such means are known from recent times (Folkard, 1870, 247; Waugh, 1919, 30).

In the early 3rd millennium BC there is evidence not only for rowing and sailing, but also for planked boats (Morrison, 1980). However, reed craft continued in use alongside them. The Bible for example records that in the mid-1st millennium BC Ethiopian ambassadors came to the Hebrews in reed craft (Isaiah, 18, 2). Rock carvings and paintings from widely separated parts of Africa – Nubia, Algerian Sahara, and Natal (Heyerdahl, 1978, 23; Vinnicombe, 1976) – may be evidence for early use outside Egypt, but dating and precise identification are difficult. Reed bundle rafts (made from bundles of *ambatch* branches, and of palm leaf mid-ribs as well as papyrus) were used this century in a great part of Africa: Atlantic Morocco, the upper Nile, White Nile, Lake Tsana, Lake Chad, Central African lakes of Kenya and Uganda, Okavango swamp and Lake Ngami in Bechuanaland (Hornell, 1970, 51-5; Worthington, 1933), and this may reflect in part the prehistoric distribution.

Boreux has argued that Egyptian reed craft were caulked or waterproofed (Casson, 1971, 13). Apart from the story of Moses, which may be based on an earlier Babylonian account (Anderson, 1978, 49), there is no Egyptian tradition of waterproofing boats with bitumen as there is in Mesopotamia. It seems likely therefore that these craft were rafts not boats, and that the scene depicts bindings being tightened.

Strabo's 1st century AD description (17.1.50) of a *pakton* made from withies resembling woven-work, which he used to cross the Nile by the first cataract, is thought by Casson (1971, 342) to refer to a skin boat, whereas Hornell (1970, 51) prefers bundle raft. As Strabo and his companions were 'standing in water or seated on small boards' a raft seems more likely than a boat, possibly a raft of *ambatch* bundles.

Log rafts   Illustrations in the tomb of Amenophis II of *c* 1500 BC (Plate 30) show rafts at *Punt*, probably on the Somali coast: they are steered by side oar and have a mast and a sail of uncertain shape. The 1st/2nd century AD *Periplus* (Chapter 7) records that rafts (almost certainly of logs) were used at *Aualites*, possibly Zeyla in Somaliland, to unload ships and to cross the Red Sea. A boat-shaped log raft made from *ambatch* limbs was in use earlier this century in Lobito Bay, Angola (Greenhill, 1976, 99, fig.48), and flat rafts are known from several regions including the Central African lakes (Worthington, 1933).

Bark boats   Hornell (1970, 183) noted one piece bark boats in Rhodesia and Tanganyika. After heating to make the bark supple, the ends were skewered or sewn and payed with clay. Simple boats such as these were practicable from an early date in this

continent but, for the present, such use must remain conjectural.

Plate 30   Representation of sailing rafts (log? or buoyed?) from the tomb of Amenophis II. Drawing after Johnstone, 1980, fig. 13.16.

Buoyed rafts   The Punt rafts (described above) may have been buoyed rafts rather than simple log rafts. However, Pliny (*HN* 6.35), from the 1st century AD, gives the first certain description of this type of craft buoyed by skin floats and used by the Ascitae, who inhabited islands off the Ethiopian coast. Rafts buoyed by pots were seen by Strabo (17.1.4) in the Nile delta; similar ones and others buoyed by gourds and by skin floats have been used in Africa in recent times, the earliest reports being from Morocco in the 18th century, and lower Egypt in the 19th (Hornell, 1970, 30–7).

Logboats   Logboats in their extended form are known from tomb carvings of 3rd millennium BC Egypt, and Heliodorus (*Aeth.* 1.31.2) mentions the use of monoxylons on the Nile delta in classical times. The *Periplus* (Chapter 15) describes logboats used for fishing from the island of *Menouthias*, probably Zanzibar or Pemba. Nineteenth century explorers found logboats in use in the upper Nile region and throughout central and southern Africa and the east and west coasts.

Logboats with double outriggers are generally in use on the east coast and the Comoro Islands, but single outriggers are used in Madagascar and on the mainland opposite. However, the double outrigger was recorded in Madagascar in the late 16th century by Houtman (Hornell, 1970, 254).

Sewn boats

The *Periplus* (Chapters 15 and 16) records the use of sewn boats from the island of *Menouthias* and at *Rhapta*, probably in the Rufiji delta south of Dar-es-Salaam. Vasco da Gama saw sewn boats at Mozambique on the same coast in 1498 and they were noted again in the late 16th century at Zanzibar by Lancaster. Hornell (1970) and others have described recent African boats with sewn planking, including the almost legendary *mtepe* from Lamu, north of Zanzibar (Plate 31). This East African tradition of sewn boats must be considered in conjunction with similar traditions in Arabia and India: an Indian Ocean phenomenon for over 2000 years.

Plate 31   Model of a *Mtepe* sewn boat. Photo: NMM.

India

Excavated material and records on clay tablets show that the great riverine civilisations of Mesopotamia and the Harappan of the Indus Valley (back endpaper) were in contact during the mid-3rd to mid-2nd millennium BC, and much of this contact is thought to have been by sea (Clark, 1977, 257, 264). About 1500 years later both Strabo (2.5.12) and the *Periplus of the Erythrean Sea* (Chapters 27, 39, 56–63) describe trading voyages between the Red Sea and the west and east coasts of India. From the 4th century AD and especially the 7th there are accounts of sea voyages between India and China (Mookerji, 1912, 165–71). Thus there was maritime intercourse from early times and, although we cannot always be certain of the country of origin of the vessels involved, one way or another Indian seamen and shipbuilders would have been exposed to influences from the Classical, Arab, Indonesian and Chinese civilisations.

The Indian sub-continent has widely differing ecological regions and many of the basic forms of raft and boat have at some time been used there.

Non-planked craft

Reed rafts   There is no tradition of waterproofing reed bundles in India and therefore rafts not boats are to be expected, and these were mentioned by Pliny (*N.H.* 6.24.82) writing in the 1st century AD: they were said to have rigging similar to that in use on the River Nile. An engraving on a seal excavated by Mackay in 1937–8 from the Harappan site at Mohenjo-Daro and an Harappan terracotta amulet

(Johnstone, 1980, 171, fig.13.1 and 13.2) may be interpreted as reed rafts as they have 'binding' lines. The first craft has high curved ends whilst the second has a low crescent-shaped outline and both have two side steering oars and a cabin-like structure amidships. Rao (1965, 36) has drawn attention to figures on two potsherds excavated from the Harappan site of Lothal, which are said to represent 'multi-oared boats', but reed rafts cannot be ruled out.

Reed bundle craft were still in use earlier this century on the Ganges and rivers in southern India (Hornell, 1970, 59–60).

Buoyed rafts and skin boats   The earliest reference to bamboo rafts buoyed by skin floats appears to be in the memoirs of Emperor Jahangir (1605–27) who used them on Kashmir rivers (Hornell, 1970, 24). They have been used in the 20th century, especially in northern India and Afghanistan (Greenhill, 1971, 140, 142, 175–6).

Tavernier recorded the mid-17th century use of round skin boats on a basket framework on rivers in central southern India (Hornell, 1970, 95, 105). Similar boats were recorded in southern India this century by Hornell (1970, Plate xv).

Earlier evidence for these two types is not known, but by comparison with other countries they are likely to have had a long history in India.

Log rafts   The *Periplus* (Chapter 60) describes rafts from the Coromandel coast, made of logs bound together. The local ones were named *sangara*; the bigger *kolandio phonta* were capable of voyages to the Ganges, Burma and South-East Asia. Log rafts of Ceylon and the Coromandel coast were drawn and described by Thomas Bowrey in the late 17th century (Hill, 1958, 209) and in this century by Hornell (1970, 61–9). They are generally known as *cata maran* ('bound logs'), but the largest rafts on the Coromandel coast are called *kola maram*, 'flying fish catamaran', a name possibly related to *kolandio*. Christie (1957) wishes to derive *kolandio* from the Chinese for 'many masted vessel': this term could be applied to the *kola maram* as these rafts have two masts with lateen sails and can stay at sea for up to three days, sailing closehauled using two leeboards and a steering oar (Plate 32). The name *sangara* may be preserved in *sangadam*, a raft used in the Laccadive Islands (Hornell, 1970, 67). In India the terms *jangar*, *jangada* and *sangadam* are now applied to paired logboats (Bowen, 1956, 287), although in Portugal and Brazil *jangada* are log rafts.

Logboats   These were mentioned by Pliny (*N.H.* 6.26 and 6.105) in the 1st century AD. They are in use in

Plate 32   A *Kolamaram*, a seven-log raft, fishing off Negapatam, southern India. After Hornell, 1970, plate XIA.

many parts of India today; some are paired (Hornell, 1970, 191) and many are extended (Greenhill, 1971).

Planked craft

Johnstone (1980, 172, 180) has drawn attention to a Chanhu-daro pottery model wheel painted to represent tripartite construction which would imply internal tenons or treenails. Furthermore, bronze gouges are known from Harappa. Thus Harappan craftsmen may have been capable of joining flush-laid boat planking by wooden fastenings, although none is known to date. A graffito on a polished potsherd from Harappan Mohenjo-Daro (Johnstone, 1980, 172, fig.13.3) is difficult to interpret, although its outline it not unlike some Egyptian representations of planked boats and may be compared with a planked boat Greenhill noted in East Pakistan this century (1971, 34). Rao (1965, 35–6) has interpreted the only complete specimen of five pottery boat models excavated from Lothal as a sailing ship (Johnstone, 1980, 173, fig.13.4) with fine bow and blunt stern. A second model is also said to have had a mast, and the other three are identified as flat-bottomed vessels with fine bows. Judgement on these interpretations must await the full publication of these finds.

The gateways to the 2nd century BC Stupa at Sanchi, India, have sculptures depicting boats, and one of these appears to have a high curved stern with a pivoted side steering oar. Mookerji (1912, 32) believes that another on the east gateway represents a sewn boat (Plate 33). This apart, there is no early evidence for sewn planked boats until the early 16th century when Barbosa noted that sewn boats annually voyaged from the Malabar coast to the Red Sea (Lane-Fox, 1875, 412–13); Balbi noted similar boats on the Coromandel coast in the late 16th century (Hill, 1958, 208). One hundred years later Bowrey (Hill, 1958, 207) recorded that the flat-bottomed

Plate 33 A sewn (?) plank boat sculptured on the 2nd century BC eastern gateway of No. 1 Stupa at Sanchi. Drawing after Mookerji, 1912, 32.

masula was 'most proper' for the surf off the Coromandel coast. These boats had broad, thin planking sewn with coir, and thwarts but no floor timbers (Plate 34). This brings to mind Strabo's (15.1.15) remark that the boats of India and Ceylon were without floor timbers (metrai). Dr Fryer, a near contemporary of Bowrey, noted that masulas were sewn with coco yarn and caulked with dammar resin. Masulas are in use on the Coromandel coast today, and Greenhill (1971) has recorded other Indian sewn boats.

The Periplus (Chapter 44) mentions trappago and kotumba used in the Gulf of Cambay, north of Bombay, to tow ships to Barugaza (probably Broach), but constructional details are not given. Two-masted ships are shown on early coins from the Coromandel coast: the Andrha coins of the 2nd/3rd centuries AD, as figured by Mookerji (1912, 50–1) have twin side steering oars, mast and yard; ships on 6th century Pallava coins appear generally similar. In outline and in rig, these craft are not unlike the 20th century sewn plank, two-masted *yathra dhoni* from Ceylon (Hornell, 1970, fig.60), but this latter vessel had head sails, a stern rudder and an outrigger.

If we discount the Lothal models the earliest knowledge of sail in Indian waters comes from Strabo (15.1.15) who reported that the sails of craft voyaging between India and Ceylon in the 1st century AD were inadequate. A three-masted ship on a fresco in cave No.2 at Ajanta, north east of Bombay (Johnstone, 1980, 185, fig.14.1) dated to *c* AD 600 has high aspect ratio sails which have been compared to those on Chinese junks. She also has a sail on an artemon-type mast, and twin side steering oars. Mookerji (1912, 42) has published a second illustration from these caves showing a boat with planking ending on a near-horizontal line and not at posts. This run of planking is similar to that on the underbody of the early 19th century *pattooa* which was clinker-built (Mookerji, 1912, 252–3), the 20th century *pallar* from East Pakistan (Greenhill, 1971, 92), and the medieval European hulc (pp. 38–40).

Plate 34   19th century drawing by Admiral Paris of a *masula* sewn boat being hauled ashore on the coast of southern India.

China

It is convenient to discuss in a single chapter the boats of Indo-China, Korea, Japan and China, an area in which there is a degree of cultural unity. Intercourse between China and the Mediterranean world and with Indian and Arab cultures, is demonstrable from Roman times (*Periplus*, Chapter 64), and contact with Indian Ocean countries and Indonesia continued, at least intermittently (Hourani, 1963, 75; Willetts, 1964; Hornell, 1970, 231; Needham, 1971, 494–6). The distinctive style of Chinese planked boat and shipbuilding seems to have received little influence from other cultures. On the other hand, the stern rudder, lee-boards, and the magnetic compass were used from an early date in the Chinese cultural area and may have been transmitted to the west.

Non-planked craft

Reed rafts   Needham (1971; 390, 396) notes that reed bundle rafts (*phu fq*) are 'not unknown' in China but does not discuss them further. There is some minor iconographic evidence, however: Nishimura (1925, 114–15, fig.33) suggested that an engraving on a possibly 3rd century BC bronze bell (*dōtaku*) may be of a reed raft.

Buoyed rafts   Nishimura (1936) believed that the legendary Japanese and Korean *uki takara* was a raft buoyed by skin floats. He has published a Ming ('late medieval') illustration of a raft buoyed by pots and propelled by oars, and Needham (1971, 387) has noted a similar device in a manuscript of AD 1044. Rafts buoyed by pots were also used on the Yellow River in the Han dynasty (200 BC–AD 200) and similar rafts buoyed by skins are in use there today.

Log rafts   Confucius, who lived during the Chou period, is said to have used a sailing raft (Needham, 1971, 396), but the earliest documentary reference to log or bamboo rafts is from 472 BC (Needham, 1971, 390). A raft mentioned in the 1st century AD appears to have had leather sides (Needham, 1971, 390).

The distinctive seagoing south-east Chinese bamboo sailing raft from Formosa/Taiwan was first mentioned in AD 1295 (Needham, 1971, 393). Today it is made of a dozen or so large bamboos lashed together and to curved thwartships bamboos so that the bottom is slightly curved transversely and longitudinally (Plate 35). A single balanced lugsail with battens is hoisted on a pole mast. The raft has two steering oars, and centre-boards are let down between the bamboos to assist steering and to reduce leeway when close-hauled. As with many other 20th century types described in this book it is not known whether this raft retains the features of its medieval namesake as there are only minimal descriptions before the recent period and the earliest illustration is dated AD 1803. By questioning Formosan sailors, Doran (1978) has documented something of the modern raft's performance. They are seakindly, unsinkable, capable of being righted if capsized, and have a useful life of up to 4 years. They can sail to within about 4 points of the wind but make best windward progress when about 6 points off. Doran estimated their maximum speed to be about 3 knots in a following wind.

A raft similar to the Formosan craft but with two or three masts and three centre-boards is found in northern Vietnam today (Needham, 1971, 393; Bowen, 1956, 288). Many other forms and sizes of raft are in regular use on Chinese rivers.

Bark boats   Nishimura (1931, 207) recorded the recent use of bark boats on the Manchurian reaches of the River Amur. He also noted in the Sappora Museum, Hokkaido, a small unprovenanced model of a birch bark canoe caulked with moss, sewn with bark fibre, and stiffened with osiers and bamboo. The Ainu of northern Japan have a tradition of bark-working and this led Nishimura (1931, 203-6) to consider they may formerly have used bark canoes.

Plate 35   Model of a Formosan raft. Photo: NMM.

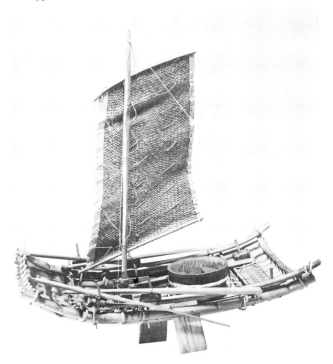

Skin boats   There are several references in Chinese literature to the round type of skin boat from the 4th century onwards (Needham, 1971, 386). A Ming dictionary defines *pi chuan* as a hide over a frame-work of bamboo or wood (Nishimura, 1931, 180), and this type of boat was used by the Monguls in their 13th century conquests (Needham, 1971, 386). Today they are used on the headwaters of the Yangtze, Yalung and Mekong and in Manchuria and Korea (Needham, 1971, 386; Hornell, 1970, 99).

The basket boats of Indo-China are a related type to these, being waterproofed with dung and oil rather than skin (Hornell, 1970, 109-11, fig.12). Some are seagoing, and a sailing version from Annam has stems and planking upperworks (Needham, 1971, 385).

Logboats   A passage in the *I Ching* has been taken to refer to the building of logboats in the 3rd millennium BC, although Needham (1971, 396) believes it may refer to fashioning planks from logs. A stone carving from the Han (*c* 200 BC–AD 200) reproduced by Worcester (1966, 3) appears to show logboats being poled and with a side steering oar, and there are references to their use in the 5th to 8th century AD literature (Needham, 1971, 392). Logboats with rectangular ends have been excavated, including ones used to contain coffins in northern Szechwan burials dated to or before the 4th century BC (Needham, 1971, 388-9; Johnstone, 1980, 187, fig.14.2). A Vietnamese logboat used in a burial of the Dông Són culture has been dated to *c* AD 375 (Bln-1438). The expansion of Cambodian logboats using fire and inserted ribs is described in a Chinese manuscript dated AD 1297 (Needham, 1971, 450).

Modern logboats are known from Japan (Nishimura, 1931, 204), Formosa (Worcester, 1956B), and from the Yalu and Yellow Rivers but they are generally rare in China (Needham, 1971, 392). Possibly the widespread use of bamboo (the giant bamboo can be 80 ft high with a diameter of 1 ft – Needham, 1971, 394), in the Chinese cultural region led early to the development of other forms of water transport at the expense of logboats. It may be, however, that logboats were a fore-runner of the dragon boats (see below).

Planked craft

Sewn boats   Needham (1971, 459) deduces from an 8th century AD document describing Malaysian sewn craft that the contemporary Chinese used iron nails and clamps to fasten planking. Whether wooden or sewn fastenings were used in earlier times cannot at present be determined, but Horridge (1978, 4) believes that some of the boats depicted on the 1st century BC Dông Són drums from Indo-China may have been sewn.

Planking was sewn in 19th century Siamese and Burmese boats (Lane-Fox, 1875, 408–12) and in some recent Thai, Vietnamese, and Ainu craft (Nishimura, 1920, 19).

Junk and sampan   The oldest representation of what might be a planked boat is the Shang (late 2nd millennium BC) pictogram *chou* = boat (Plate 36). This element is also contained in contemporary pictograms for *ship*, *to transport*, *to caulk a seam*, and *to propel by oar*.

Plate 36
Chinese pictogram for 'boat'.

Plate 37
Chinese pictogram for 'sail'.

A fragmented wooden tomb model from Changsha dated to *c* 49 BC (Needham, 1971, 447, fig.961) seems to have overhanging punt-shaped ends and a flat bottom. No bulkheads are apparent, but there is a notch in one end for a steering sweep. Two pottery boat models of the 1st century AD excavated in the 1950s from tombs near Canton (Needham, 1971, 448, figs.962 to 5, 1036–7) have a similar shape, being square-ended and flat-bottomed. No bulkheads are visible in the photographs published by Needham, but one model has poling galleries along the sides (a feature of later river boats) and a median rudder slung under the overhanging stern (the earliest evidence for this).

There is no early direct evidence for sail, but a pictogram indicates that sail was used from the late 2nd millennium BC (Plate 37) and Needham (1971, 601) believes that a 3rd century AD text indicates that southern Chinese ships had fore and aft, matting sails. Mast and sail are shown on a 6th century AD stone stele sculpture in a temple at Chengtu (Needham, 1971, 457, fig.970) but this is a square sail not the fore and aft 'traditional' Chinese lugsail. Vessels on frescoes in the cave temples at Tunhuang (Needham, 1971, 455) which are steered by a side steering oar also have square sails. The 7th century AD ships shown on the fresco at Ajanta, India, have high aspect ratio (possibly lug) sails on three masts radiating like a fan, traditionally associated with the Chinese, but other aspects of these ships appear to be from other traditions. An unusual ship in the series depicted on the late 8th century temple reliefs of Borobodur, Java, evidently has a lugsail with the matting texture indicated (Needham, 1971, 458, fig. 974b). Needham claims this to be the 'oldest representation of a Chinese seagoing ship'. It is certainly different from other ships depicted at Borobodur (see p.63) in having no outrigger and only one mast, but none of its features, apart from the sail, seem to be typically 'Chinese'. On the other hand, a ship carved on the Bayon at Angkor Thom, Cambodia, dated AD 1185 (Needham, 1971, fig.975), which is also different from adjacent ones, has several distinctive features: overhanging stern with median axial rudder and two masts with Chinese-type battened sails and multiple sheets. It is not clear whether there are transom ends, and obviously any bulkheads cannot be seen (both important diagnostic features) but such imprecision is inevitable with iconographic evidence.

A late 14th century river craft excavated from a tributary of the Yellow River (Plate 38) is transom-ended, with 13 bulkheads, fittings for a slung rudder, the remains of two masts and poling walkways. This is the first significant evidence for what has come to be thought of as the Chinese tradition of ship-building.

In the late 13th century Marco Polo described large four-masted seagoing ships. They had iron-fastened, double-thickness pine or fir planking caulked with oakum and payed with a mixture of lime, hemp and oil. Some of the larger ships had 13 watertight bulkheads (Needham, 1971, 466–8). Fifty years later the Arab geographer Ibn Battutah (Needham, 1971, 469) described *jonqs* with four

decks and sails of battened matting. From his account we can deduce that the sequence of building was:
1 Bottom planking (not specifically mentioned)
2 Lower side planking
3 Bulkheads.
The method of fastening the planking is not described but this appears to be a form of shell building with bulkheads determining the run of the upper side planking but not the lower. A similar sequence was recorded in AD 1637 when it was said to be akin to the methods used in the early 15th century (Needham, 1971, 410–16). In the early 20th century, the bulkheads were also inserted before the side planking had been completed and thus determined the form of at least part of the sides, nevertheless the planks were edge-fastened (Audemard, 1957).

Needham (1971, 409) notes the interesting fact that in AD 1158 Chang Chung-Yan made a small 'demonstration model' before building a ship. This may be a reference to a method of getting the form of a vessel from a model, although Needham (1971, 413) emphasises that traditional Chinese building was 'by eye'.

Some of the features characteristic of recent

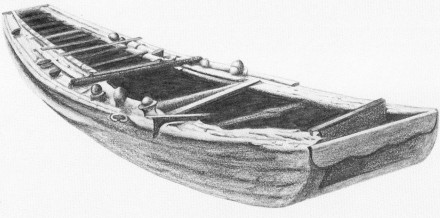

Plate 38   A river boat excavated from a tributary of the Yellow River and dated AD 1377. Drawing after Needham, 1971, fig. 979.

Chinese shipbuilding can be recognised in early times: the general form with flat, keel-less bottom and bluff bow and bluff overhanging stern; the median rudder; poling gallery; and stern sculling, all from the 1st centuries BC/AD. Others are later: multiple masts, 3rd century AD; lee-boards, 8th century; battened lugsails and multiple sheets, 12th century. And it is not until descriptions from 13th/14th century western travellers can be integrated with the evidence from the excavated 14th century river craft (Plate 38) that the individual characteristics come together in a recognisable Chinese tradition. When this is combined with the mid-17th century testimony of Sung Ying-Hsing (Needham, 1971, 410–16) we can visualise a ship similar to those known in recent times (Plate 39). It thus seems possible that, as has happened elsewhere, there was more than one type of planked craft and more than one sail form in use in pre-13th century China, and that the building tradition which came to be dominant acquired features from more than one source.

Plate 39　A 19th century drawing by Admiral Paris of a small junk at Macao.

Plate 40　A craft (possibly a dragon boat) depicted on the Dông Són drums from Indo-China. Drawing after Needham, 1971, fig. 960.

This construction with bulkheads at intervals along the length has been compared to a longitudinally split bamboo stem stiffened by nodes (Needham, 1971, 389-91), but as there is no firm evidence for bulkheads before the late 13th century AD a prehistoric origin for this concept is not proven. On the other hand, the run of the bottom planking of 20th century junks has similarities with the curved logs of Formosan rafts, and Needham (1971, 395) has drawn attention to a 3rd/4th century AD Chinese tradition that the junk was indeed developed from the raft.

Dragon boats   A planked boat (*lung chuan*), different from the junk/sampan tradition, is now widespread in the Chinese cultural area. These craft, known as dragon boats, are relatively long with overhanging ends supported by a hogging truss, and have 36 or more paddlers. Their principal element is a central longitudinal member, either a keel or an internal keelson into which 'rudimentary bulkheads' are slotted (Needham, 1971, 437; Worcester, 1965A). Other construction details are not published. Dragon boats are known from 3rd century AD Cambodia and Cochin–China (Needham, 1971, 450) and in recent times from Siam and Burma. What may be early representations of this type are depicted on some of the Dông Són drums (Plate 40) which have a wide distribution in South-East Asia.

Needham believes the dragon boats to be 'canoe-derivatives' in a 'world of raft-derivatives'. True or not, the distinction does emphasise the necessity to be alert for Chinese plank boatbuilding not in the 'mainstream' junk tradition. Such evidence may indicate diversity in former times, and there are signs of this not only in the dragon boat tradition but also in the keel-less 'snake-boats' of the River Kungthan, which have no bulkheads, and the boats from southwest Yunnan, also without bulkheads but with frames (Needham, 1971, 437).

Indonesia

Water transport would have been essential in this vast archipelago (in which I include Malaysia and the Philippines) from at least the times of rising sea level some 12000 years ago. The region does not have the long tradition of literacy that exists in China and thus textual evidence is thin until 'first contact' with post-medieval European man in the early 16th century. From early times the region has influenced and been influenced by Indian and Chinese cultures and this may be reflected to some extent in shipbuilding.

Non planked craft

Log rafts   Rafts have been used in the Philippines (Paris, 1843) and on Indonesian lakes in recent times (Hornell, 1970, 41, 70), and linguistic evidence points to their early use in Java and the Philippines (Haddon and Hornell, 1938, 15). Use elsewhere is possible but has not been noted.

Bark boats   Bark boats with sewn ends caulked with clay and with light transverse timbers were used by the Borneo Dyaks in the 19th century (Nishimura, 1931, 225).

Logboats   Simple logboats including some with stabilisers (Dumont d'Urville, 1834) have been used in recent times on sheltered waters in this region, and boats of this type have been excavated from the Niah caves in Borneo, but dating and details of construction are not yet available (Johnstone, 1980, fig.15.10). A logboat in a *c* 2nd century AD (BM–959) boat burial near Selinsing, Malaya, excavated by Sieveking (1954), had a series of pierced cleats at intervals across the inside–probably for inserted ribs. This could mean that the boat had been extended or expanded. Logboats expanded by heat were in recent use in Malaya and Burma (Sieveking, 1954, 210; Johnstone, 1980, 212), and undated paintings in the Niah caves may show extended logboats (Johnstone, 1980, fig.15.9). Detached timbers found with the Selinsing boat may be the remains of an outrigger.

Planked craft

Boats with outriggers In recent times the double outrigger boat has been dominant in Indonesia, Malaya and the Philippines, although single outriggers were seen at first contact (Haddon and Hornell, 1938, 18). The boats of the early 20th century were planked on a (vestigial) logboat base, the flush-laid strakes being edge-fastened by treenails; inserted ribs were lashed to cleats projecting from the planking and to superposed crossbeams, thus clamping the planks together.

Horridge (1978) has recently attempted to document the features of one of the several named types of double outrigger craft, the Moluccan *kora kora*, and from accounts dated between 1544 and 1668 the following characteristics emerge:
FORM Of galley proportions, double ended with high extremities and rockered keel.
STRUCTURE Logboat base with planking fastened flush by treenails in thickness of planking. Shell sequence with light flexible ribs lashed to cleats proud of planking and to crossbeams which protrude through the sides and support outrigger platforms.
PROPULSION AND STEERING Paddlers on crossbeams and on outrigger platforms. A single side steering oar.

The 1544 account quoted by Horridge (1978) states that *kora kora* were not sailed and either end could be used as bow; and the *kora kora* illustrated by de Bry (1601, vol.5, plate XVI) is propelled by paddlers on two platforms on both outriggers (Plate 41). Drawings of other double outrigger craft dated *c*1680 and *c*1798 published by Horridge (1978, fig.5) show bipod, or possibly tripod, masts towards one end, and the 1798 boat has a canted rectangular sail with boom: both have paddlers on outriggers and the 1680 boat also has paddlers or rowers inboard. A drawing published by Paris (1843, plate 104) shows a *kora kora* with canted, boomed rectangular sails on two pole masts. This type of sail seems to be indigenous as it appears on early drawings of other Indonesian craft (Plate 42) and the 1544 account describes sails of sackcloth or matting. Paddled craft with outriggers, other than *kora kora*, are illustrated in early drawings, and the 1544 account mentions several type names: further work is required to determine whether these were distinct types or variations of one building tradition.

The late 8th century sculptures on the Buddhist temple at Borobodur, Java, include representations of five boats with outriggers (Plate 43). They are double-ended with high extremities, have a side

Plate 41 A 16th century drawing of a *coracora* and other craft seen off Banda in the Moluccas. From de Bry, 1601, plate XVI.

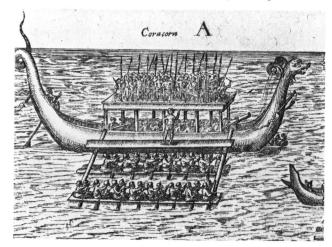

steering oar and outriggers probably on both sides, and the superstructure appears to be a framework of poles. Four of them have two main sails and a 'bowsprit', the sails being canted, rectangular on bipod (or possibly tripod) masts. Double outrigger craft may thus have been used in Indonesian waters from the 8th century until first European contact, but further evidence is required to make this more than a supposition.

Craft without outriggers A radiocarbon date of *c* AD 293 (BM–958) has recently been obtained for fragments of sewn planking found at Pontian, Malaya, in 1925. Boats of sewn planks were built in the late 17th century Philippines (Horridge, 1978, 11) and in 19th century Malaya, the Moluccas (Lane-Fox, 1875, 411–12) and Borneo (Folkard, 1870, 261), possibly indicating a tradition in this region which may pre-date the use of treenail plank fastenings.

A recent fragmentary find near Hong Kong has the planking fastened by treenails within the plank thickness, akin to the method used for the *kora kora* boat, with laths metal-nailed along the join. Some of the planking has carved integral cleats which may be rib lashing points (Hin and Ng, 1974). The find is dated *c* 1290 ± 80 ad and some of the artifacts recovered may be from Thailand/Malaya (Peacock, personal communication), but their degree of association with the planking is uncertain and in any case they do not necessarily indicate a Malay/Indonesian origin for the boat.

Boat fragments excavated in 1953 from Johore Lama, Malaya, and considered by the excavator to be an 18th or 19th century *perahu pukat* (Sieveking, 1954, 229–30), have the strakes edge-fastened not only by treenails but also by draw-tongue joints held in place by other treenails at right angles. On the other hand, Wallace noted that 19th century Malayan *prahau* had stitched planking (Lane–Fox, 1875, 411).

The early 20th century *orembai* (Plate 44) of the Moluccas and adjacent islands was shell built with flush-laid planking fastened by treenails, and ribs

Plate 42   A late 16th century drawing of craft seen in the Banda Sea. From de Bry, 1629, plate XXIIX.

Plate 43   Relief on a late 8th century AD frieze on the Buddhist temple at Borobodur, Java. Photo: David Attenborough.

lashed to cleats left proud of the planking with curves generally achieved by hewing rather than bending (Hornell, 1970, 207-8). The sea Dyak boat of Borneo (Christie, 1957, 350) and the *prahu belang* of Aru Island (Horridge, 1978, 24-30) were similarly built, thus emphasising how widespread this technique was. These boats have no outriggers and probably represent a distinctive Indonesian tradition, for boats without outriggers but capable of carrying 50 or more men are mentioned in the 'first contact' account of 1544 cited by Horridge (1978, 10). *Perahus* are also mentioned in this account as one of several types of Moluccan boat used for fishing and as ships boats. Subsequent accounts mentioning this term give insufficient details for the characteristic features to be identified. *Prahu* is now a general term for boat in South-East Asia and it is unwise to link it with any specific traditions of boatbuilding.

Chinese and other influences   Needham (1971, 458-9) has noted a mid-8th century AD Chinese description of sailing ships which seem to have been Malayan. They were divided by bulkheads into three sections and coconut fibre was used to fasten the planking, which was of several thicknesses. Thus they seem to have had some Chinese features in a Malayan sewn hull. Moluccan cargo ships known as *sampan* are

mentioned in the 1544 account, and *junco* ships from Java with 3 or 4 layers of planking were reported by Barbosa in the early 16th century (Hill, 1958, 203). Ships off the Moluccas, Manilla and Java with Chinese-type battened lugsails (Plate 42) are illustrated by de Bry (1629, 1602, 1619) and Linschoten (1610): they lack many of the generally accepted features of Chinese shipping, but some have the characteristic Indonesian side steering oars as do the ships with canted rectangular sails with booms seen on Plate 42. Further research is required to establish whether these may be indigenous Indonesian traditions.

Di Varthema wrote of a *fusta*, an early 16th century oared vessel, in the Bay of Bengal and this term is subsequently mentioned regularly in English and Dutch records (Hill, 1958, 203-5). De Bry (1629, plate XXVII) illustrated a Javanese *fusta* with two masts, and a vessel of similar form is illustrated by Linschoten (1610, 78) off Malabar. These drawings show a mixture of features difficult to identify with any known South-East Asian tradition, and Hill (1958, 205) argues from documentary evidence for the *fusta* being a European type. This highlights the difficulty of determining what is truly indigenous in 16th and 17th century reports.

Plate 44   An *orembai* of Ternate, Moluccas. Drawing after Hornell, 1970, plate XXXII.

Australia

The aboriginal population of Australia is thought to have come from the islands to the south-east of Asia. At periods of low sea level the Sunda shelf connected western Indonesia to mainland South-East Asia, and the Sahul shelf connected New Guinea and adjacent islands to Australia; nevertheless there was open water to be crossed (Clark, 1977, 454) as deep channels existed in the region of the Wallace and the Weber lines (front endpaper). Man entered the continent of Australia sometime before 40 000 BC (Mulvaney, 1975), and two possible routes have been suggested: a northern route from Borneo to New Guinea with a chain of islands between the two mainlands (longest gap *c* 80 km); and a southern route from Java to Australia with islands in between (longest gap *c* 100 km).

The tool kit of the earliest Australians consisted of scrapers and simple percussion and bone tools (Clark, 1977, 24). These were later supplemented by points and backed blades, possibly as a result of further immigration about 3000 BC, but these supplementary tools have not been found in Tasmania, probably because of isolation by rising sea level before *c* 10 000 BC (Clark, 1977, 463–5). Tasmanian technology proved to be conservative and there was little, if any, subsequent contact with Australia until after the first European contact in the 17th/18th centuries AD. Thus Tasmanian water transport at first contact may give an indication of that used by the earliest immigrants to the continent.

In late prehistoric times boats from New Guinea and the Celebes visited northern Australia. However, the Australian aborigines never adopted agriculture and, although logboats were probably introduced at this time, other aspects of technology do not seem to have been changed by these contacts with Neolithic societies (Shutler, 1975, 42–4). Thus the range of watercraft used in mainland Australia at first European contact may be representative of that used during the previous 5000 years.

Non-planked craft

Reed rafts   Birdsell (1977, 135) quotes an early report from Tasmania of rafts of five bundles of rushes lashed together. Their performance was similar to that of bark rafts.

Bark rafts and boats   Hornell (1970, 182–6) has surveyed the evidence for early bark craft and his work may be supplemented by Birdsell's (1977) recent research.

Three types of bark craft were probably in use at first contact:
BARK RAFTS used by Tasmanians (not otherwise known). They were made of bark from the tea-tree shrub or eucalyptus (*E. obliqua*). Three tapering bundles were bound by grass ropes and lashed together with upturned ends. The two smaller bundles were lashed above and outboard of the bigger bundle thus forming a 'boat shape' (Roth, 1899, 155). These rafts could carry 7 to 8 people and were paddled or poled on rivers and out to coastal islands over distances of about 16 km. They had to be dried-out after 5–6 hours use (Plate 2).
SIMPLE BARK BOATS were used in still waters in the Murray–Darling basin. Troughs were made from a

thick sheet of bark of the red gum (*Eucalyptus camaldulensis*) and the open ends blocked with clay.
LASHED BARK BOATS were used in the rivers and creeks of New South Wales and south-eastern Victoria. A thin bark sheet of *Eucalyptus obliqua* was heated over a fire until pliable; the ends were then pleated, bunched together and tied with bark cord and a supporting framework of saplings and pliant ribs inserted (Plate 45). This was potentially a better boat than the open-ended type but it similarly became waterlogged after prolonged use.
SEWN BARK BOATS were used on the Queensland coast and the northern coast of Australia. Built from one or more sheets of eucalyptus bark sewn together and caulked with gum, sheer was obtained at the pointed ends by sewing on extra bark strips. These boats were known to be used for a 32 km passage in open water (Birdsell, 1977, 138).

Log rafts　Three types of log raft were used by the mainland Australians (Hornell, 1970; 71–2; Birdsell, 1977); there are no reports of their use in Tasmania.
RIVER RAFTS　Mangrove saplings lashed together, often temporarily, were used in eastern Queensland.
SINGLE RAFT　On the southern portion of the Gulf of Carpentaria light mangrove saplings about 10 ft in length were joined together by hardwood pegs or lashings to make a trapezoidal form.
DOUBLE RAFT　The *kalum* was used off shore and in the estuaries of Australia's north-west coast, and consisted of two single rafts, one of 7 poles partly overlapping one of 9 poles with their narrow ends towards the centre. They were used on crossings of over 16 km for island exploration.

Logboats　Melanesian and Indonesian influence prior to first European contact is thought to have resulted in the introduction of logboats and sail to the north Australia coast. Outrigger craft were seen by Cook off Cape York Peninsular during his first voyage (Best, 1925, 201).

Prehistoric use

The bark, reed and log rafts and the bark boats described above were all built with a simple percussion and bone toolkit. They would have been adequate for Aboriginal inland travel and exploitation of the environment. In their recent form, however,

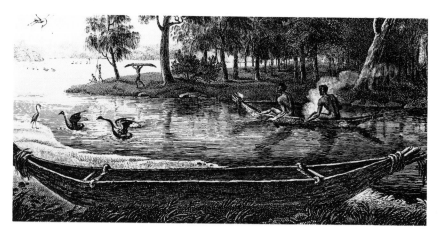

Plate 45　Drawing of an early 19th century Australian lashed bark boat from Lesueur and Petit's Atlas to Peron's *Voyage of Discovery*.

they are probably not suitable for a 80 km channel crossing: this is particularly applicable to the reed and bark rafts of the Tasmanians who are thought to be technologically similar to the first immigrants. It may be, however, that technological reversion had occurred when, without the stimulus of a requirement for sea voyages and in the possible absence of the optimum raw material, the art of building substantial craft was lost. Such a 'regression' occurred during the last few centuries before European contact, the so-called 'Adaptive Phase', when the number and variety of stone tools evidently decreased in some parts of Australia (Shutler, 1975, 37).

Log rafts and reed rafts of advanced form but of simple technology can be used for sea voyages – see p.76 and Heyerdahl's replicas *Kon Tiki* and *Ra*. The logs have to be relatively lightweight and both logs and reeds must be of a species which does not readily become waterlogged. Bark boats have been known to make limited sea voyages (see p.78); bark rafts are unknown outside Tasmania. To be other than a drift voyage, methods of propulsion and steering would need to be evolved.

Birdsell (1977, 143-4) has pointed out that bamboo is available along the hypothetical northern migration route, and this has been used for rafts in New Guinea and several Melanesian islands in recent times (Hornell, 1970, 70-4). East of Java, on the southern route, where there is relatively low rainfall, there appears to be no bamboo (Birdsell, 1977, 144) but other raft timber grows in Indonesia. Two eucalypts (*deglupta* and *alba*) grow today on at least portions of the two routes but their suitability for bark rafts or boats has not been demonstrated (Birdsell, 1977, 142-3), however boats, of an unknown species of bark, were used in Borneo in the 19th century (p.61).

The earliest inhabitants of Australia probably arrived by raft, but which type of raft is by no means clear.

Oceania

The Neolithic forebears of the population of Melanesia (New Guinea and the islands north-east of Australia) had spread from South-East Asia to New Caledonia before 3000 BC (Bellwood, 1978, 46). The occupation of Micronesia (coral atolls north of Melanesia and east of the Philippines) is not so well-documented but dates so far obtained are in the mid-2nd millenium BC. The generally accepted view about the settlement of Polynesia, which extends from Melanesia to Hawaii in the north, Easter Island in the east and New Zealand in the south, is that movement was from the Philippines and eastern Indonesia through Melanesia to reach Fiji during the 2nd millennium BC (Bellwood, 1978, 45-6; Shutler, 1975, 79); thence to occupy the 'many islands' from the west. This is supported to a degree by the spread of radiocarbon dates, the latest ones being c 4th century AD for Hawaii and Easter Island, and 11th century AD for New Zealand (Clark, 1977, 488, table 31 and Shulter, 1975, 80). Heyerdahl's minority view (1978, 146-7) is that there was a Neolithic movement from eastern Asia or the Philippines to the west coast of America, using the eastward flowing Kuroshiwo current. Subsequently, currents flowing westwards from central and south America brought migrants to Samoa, and south-westerly flowing currents brought further migrants from Hawaii to central Polynesia.

Europeans came into contact with Oceania from the 16th century but as the islands are spread over a vast ocean some were not encountered until the 19th century (front endpaper). Reports made at first contact are the main source of evidence for boats, together with oral tradition. Haddon and Hornell

(1936–8) recorded details of the many boat types in use in the early 20th century, and collected together some of these first contact reports.

Non-planked craft

Reed rafts The New Zealand Maori are the only recent users of reed rafts in Oceania, although Heyerdahl (1972, 20) notes a tradition of their former use on Easter Island. The Maori temporary rafts, *mokihi*, were made from bound bulrushes (*raupo*, *Typha angustifolia*) or flax (*Phormium*), and ranged in size from one-man sit-astride models to boat-shaped ones of 5 bundles (Best, 1925, 140, fig.100). They were used to cross rivers by paddling or poling. All reports indicate that the reed soon became water-logged.

Buoyed rafts The late-19th century Moriori of the Chatham Islands, south-east of New Zealand, had a wooden framework, boat-shaped raft with extra buoyancy from dry fernstems and rolls of flax stalks packed against the bottom and sides (Hornell, 1970, 38–9). The larger rafts also had inflated bladders of bull kelp (*rimu*) and were used for inter-island journeys up to 12 miles. Hornell recorded that they were propelled by oar, but this may have been after European influence.

Log rafts Log rafts were noticed at first contact in several places: Quiros, in Marquesas Island in 1595, probably referred to them (Hornell, 1970, 79); Cook saw them in New Zealand in 1773 (Best, 1925, 137); and Beachey in Mangareva Island in 1825 (Hornell, 1970, 77). These latter were seagoing and had a sail (Plate 4).

Hornell (1970, 75–9) concluded from the 20th century widely dispersed use of rafts and legends of their former use that there was 'considerable evidence in favour of the great antiquity of raft navi-

gation' in Polynesia. This 20th century distribution includes: Marquesas and Mangareva in eastern Polynesia, Society Islands in the central region, and New Zealand in the south-west. Rafts were also used from eastern New Guinea throughout Melanesia, but reports of Micronesian rafts have not been traced. Hornell (1970, 73–7) noted that in recent times rafts had apparently replaced logboats in New Zealand, New Ireland and in the Torres Island; and in Mangareva rafts had recently replaced paired logboats. Thus the 20th century distribution does not necessarily reflect ancient practice.

The rafts reported varied in constructional details with no obvious regional pattern. Some were 'shaped', with a narrow forward end (Fiji); some were rectangular (New Hebrides); in some the elements were lashed together directly (New Ireland) or with transverse timbers (Mangareva), or pinned with wooden pegs (Solomon Islands). The majority were of (unspecified) logs, but some were of bamboo (Fiji, New Hebrides, Bismark Archipelago – all in Melanesia). All were paddled but the rafts of Mangareva were also sailed; uniquely, rafts of the Society Islands are said to have been towed by kite (Hornell, 1970, 71–8). Some rafts had side railings but most seem to have not; Fiji rafts sometimes had thatched huts. Another unusual feature is that the Santa Cruz Island Melanesian raft recorded by Paris (1843, Plate 114) had an outrigger. New Zealand rafts of the mid-19th century (Best, 1925, 136, fig.97) were made of two sets of two-tiered softwood logs pinned together, the sets being joined at 3 to 5 feet apart by three transverse poles.

In early 20th century eastern New Guinea, *lakatoi*, rafts made of five or more logboats lashed to transverse members which supported a platform of saplings on which huts were erected, were used for trading within a group of islands (Best, 1925, 260–1). Rudolph (1974, 199, fig.147) figures one with two sails. Since European first contact, Oceanic rafts have been known to undertake only short voyages; for example, the Mangarevans travelled up to 30 miles in a single voyage (Hornell, 1970, 77).

Logboats Basic un-extended logboats are scarcely noted in Oceanic accounts, but this may be because they were overlooked. Thompson (Best, 1925, 260) recorded recent use on the rivers of New Guinea, where they were poled, and Best (1925, 5, 6, 22) claimed that simple logboats (*waka tiwa*) were much used 'in former times' in calm New Zealand waters.

Planked craft

Although some early reports mention 'keels', it seems probable that, at first contact, the central longitudinal member of Oceanic planked boats was of logboat hull form. See, for example, Banks' drawing of a *pahi* of the Society Islands (Greenhill, 1976, 28, fig.1). Thus they were to some degree 'extended logboats', the logboat base being less prominent in some than others.

There were differences in detail, but the following general building method seems to hold:

1 Tree felled by stone axes and head burned off.
2 Top side of log levelled to intended sheerline and required outline sketched on it.
3 Log hollowed using fire and adze; boat shaped externally at bow and stern.
4 When log was of insufficient length, other logs were hollowed and joined end to end by sewing with roots or fibre using butted or more complex joints. Similarly, where height at ends was insufficient, bow and stern pieces were added.
5 Other logs were split, using fire and hardwood wedges; the resultant planks were finished with an adze.
6 Washstrakes fitted to obtain the height required. They were sewn edge-to-edge, sometimes through holes in the planking, sometimes through projections from the planking, holes being made by pointed bones. Where there was more than one plank per strake, they were butted. Seams were filled with, for example, dried rushes, and were sometimes rein-

Plate 46   An early 19th century Maori war canoe. After Best, 1925.

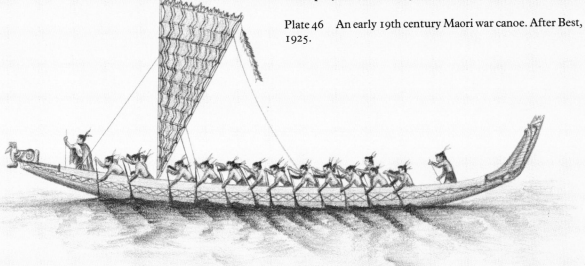

forced by longitudinal laths. Hull and seams were payed with resin (Best, 1925, 38-9, 71-2, 217, 228).

7 In certain boats ribs were inserted and lashed to cleats left proud of the planking or direct to the planking (Hornell, 1970, 207-9).

8 Crossbeam/thwarts were fitted in the bigger boats.

Single boats Single boats without outriggers, were encountered in New Zealand, Tonga, Paumota, and the Austral, Society and Solomon Islands (Rienits, 1968, 43; Best, 1925, 10, 23, 35, 190, 257-8; Bellwood, 1978, fig.12; Hornell, 1970, 209). The reports and drawings are of the 'war canoe' type of boat with prominent vertical ends, especially the stern (Plate 46). Twentieth century New Zealand use of smaller and simpler boats (*waka tete*) of the same basic construction, for coastal fishing (Best, 1925,

Plate 47   Drawing of a paired boat seen by LeMaire and Schouten off Tafahi, Tonga, in 1616.

5-6) may indicate that similar ones were used at an earlier date in Oceania but were not documented by Europeans. The Solomon Islands *mon*, similar to the Moluccan *orembai* but with sewn washstrakes, is possibly a 20th century successor to this type of boat (Haddon and Hornell, 1938, 39-40).

Paired boats Two single logboats were connected laterally by two or more transverse beams or poles lashed to each boat (Plate 47). The units in the pair were separated by 2 to 8 feet and thus achieved an effective beam of 6 to 15 feet thereby increasing lateral stability (McGrail, 1978, 45-51). A platform was built on top of the transverse beams and sometimes a mast was stepped there. Generally, the two hulls seem to have been roughly the same length, but differences in length up to 15 ft (20 per cent) have been noted in New Zealand, Fiji and neighbouring islands in recent times (Best, 1925, 13, 203, 205, 241; Haddon and Hornell, 1938, 42).

Paired boats were seen in great numbers by the first Europeans: Banks saw 'some hundreds' near East Cape, New Zealand in 1769; and Forster counted 159 paired 'war canoes' from 50ft to 90ft long and 70 smaller canoes, most of them paired ones, at Tahiti in 1774 during Cook's second voyage (Best, 1925, 23, 222-3). By the time that Vancouver visited Tahiti in 1792 he saw no such boats and noted that land warfare had replaced fighting at sea (Best, 1925, 35).

Early reports (Best, 1925) of these boats were from:

POLYNESIA   Tuamotu (1616), New Zealand (1642), Tonga (1643), Tahiti (1769), Hawaii (1777), Cook (1777), Samoa (1786), Austral (1791).
MELANESIA   Santa Cruz (1595), New Caledonia (1773), Fiji (1827).
MICRONESIA   Carolines (1830).

Boats with outriggers Except for the New Guinea region of Melanesia (Dumont d'Urville, 1835, Plate XXII) early reports of boats with double outriggers have not been traced, although Maori legend appears to describe their use (Best, 1925, 17); and there are references to their use in recent times in Nissan Islands, Samoa, Easter Island, New Guinea and the Louisiade Archipelago (Best, 1925, 17, 201, 260).

The single outrigger has been by far the most popular Oceanic form in recent times and there are early reports from all parts of the area (Best, 1925; Haddon and Hornell, 1936-8):

POLYNESIA Marquesas (1595), Tonga (1643), Easter Island (1722), Tahiti (1767), New Zealand (1769), Hawaii (1777), Samoa (1786), Austral (1791).
MELANESIA Santa Cruz (1793), Admiralty (1798), Fiji (1827).
MICRONESIA Ladrones (1521), Carolines (1530).

The smaller boats were paddled; others were sailed, steered by stern sweep. Outrigger assemblages varying in size, shape and structure have been studied in some detail by Haddon and Hornell (1936-1938).

Use of an outrigger is one of several ways of improving the lateral stability of a long, narrow logboat or logboat-based boat (McGrail, 1978, 51-5). This is achieved by increasing the effective beam, in this case with only a slight increase in resistance to motion. Thus, this is a design of high speed potential, and high speed under paddle or sail was in fact frequently commented on by early Europeans.

The double-ended sailing *proa*, *prau* or *proe* was especially noted for speed in early Micronesian reports. This craft had an asymmetric transverse section being rounded on one side and flat on the other, which was thought to reduce leeway. In reports dated between 1521 and 1841, the outrigger was noted to be on the rounded side of the boat; however there is not such unanimity about the mode of operation. Magellan (1521), Anson (1742) and Morrell (1830) claimed that the outrigger was kept to windward, whilst Dampier (1686) and Crozet (1772) said to leeward (Best, 1925; Haddon and Hornell, 1936). Dampier and Morrell also describe how the boat was 'shunted' to change tack. 'Shunting' is only necessary in single outrigger craft when it is used to ensure that the outrigger remains to windward: in double-ended boats with the mast amidships the tack of the sail is moved from the bow to the stern, which then becomes the bow. However, from the 17th and 18th century evidence cited above it seems that Marianas and Carolines boats could be used with the outrigger either to windward or to leeward, and this is indeed what is shown on an illustration (Plate 48) of Dutch ships and Ladrones (Marianas) craft published by de Bry (1619, vol.11, Plate XV). Two hundred years later, Paris (1843, Plate 107) figured two Carolines boats, one with the outrigger to windward and one with it to leeward (Plate 49): the latter condition is potentially unstable and to counteract this a balance board is being used on the windward side. Dumont d'Urville (1835, Plate LIX) also illustrated the use of balance boards in the Carolines in 1827. Single outrigger craft with balance boards were seen in the Society Islands during Cook's visit in 1767 (Best, 1925, 218), and the technique has been reported from 19th century Samoa, New Guinea and the Solomons (Lane-Fox, 1875, 430) where the single outrigger craft have definite bow and stern and therefore cannot 'shunt' but must tack, thus alternately bringing the outrigger to leeward. Greenhill (1971, 124) figures a 20th century Pakistan *ekdar hora* with single outrigger to leeward, opposed by a balance board, a configuration in which the boat can be sailed closer to the wind than with outrigger to windward (1971, 157): this may explain similar use in the Micronesian boats.

Plate 48   An early 17th century drawing of Dutch ships and local craft off the Ladrones Islands (Marianas). From de Bry, 1619, plate xv.

Plate 49   Single outrigger craft with balance boards in the Caroline Islands, drawn by Admiral Paris.

Regional traditions   The three regions of Oceania are defined principally on geographical grounds, but also partly for racial and cultural reasons. Doran (1973, 42, fig. 30) has argued for comparable groupings of certain nautical traits: the form of hull, the sail, and tacking procedures. An analysis of first contact reports could reveal the state before European influence, but some of these accounts give insufficient detail and some illustrations appear 'to have been worked up at home' (Haddon and Hornell, 1938, 18) and thus may be inaccurate. The analysis has therefore been extended to the time of Admiral Paris' work in the early 19th century, balancing the risk of European influence against gains in accuracy and depth of reports.

Following Haddon and Hornell (1938, 45–54) Oceanic sails are today conventionally classified as 'sprit' (Plate 46), 'lateen' (Plate 47) or 'rectangular', although they differ in form, rigging and use from European sails with these names. An agreed analytical nomenclature for non-European sails is urgently needed: in its absence the conventional terminology is used in Table 2.

Where a craft is sighted is not necessarily her region of origin, and the later reports in this small sample may be unrepresentative of 'first contact'. Nevertheless tentative conclusions may be drawn from Table 2 about the pre-European state:

POLYNESIA   Single boats, paired boats, single outrigger boats, and a log raft were sailed in this region. Lateen sails were used in eastern Polynesia with one case in New Zealand and one in Mangareva; sprits were used in northern, central and southern Polynesia. Although tacking predominated, 'shunting' (*fide* Cook) was undertaken around Tonga.

MICRONESIA   Single outrigger boats with lateen sails were 'shunted': the outrigger might be used to leeward (*fide* Dampier and Crozet), probably counteracted by balance board.

MELANESIA   Double outrigger, single outrigger and paired boats had lateen or canted rectangular sails. Except for the 'shunting' of paired Fijian boats operations are insufficiently documented.

Table 2   Hull form, sail, and tacking procedures in Oceania up to the early 19th century

Sources: Best, 1925, 27–8, 182, 217–18, 227, 232–3, 236, 239–40, 246–9, 254, 261–2, 264–5.
Dumont d'Urville, 1835, plates V, XXII, LIX.
Rudolph, 1974, 40, 91, 111–12.
Rienits, 1968, 43, 99.
Haddon and Hornell, 1936, figs. 2, 21a, 86, 130, 189, 190, 192, 193.
Hornell, 1970, 77.
Paris, 1843, plates 106–19.

Polynesia

		Craft	Sail	Mast	Tack/Shunt
Tonga	1616	Paired boat	Lateen	Forward	Tack
New Zealand	1642	Paired boat	Lateen	Forward?	?
Tonga	1643	Paired boat	Lateen	Forward?	?
Society Is.	1767	Single Outrigger	Sprit	Amidships	?†
New Zealand	1769	Single boat	Sprit	Forward	Tack
Tonga	1774	Paired boat	Lateen	Amidships	Shunt
Tonga	1774	Paired boat	Lateen?	Forward	Tack
Tonga	1777	Paired boat	Lateen	Amidships	?
Tonga	1777	Single Outrigger	Lateen?	Amidships?	?†
Society Is.	1777	Single Outrigger	Sprit	Amidships?	?†
Hawaii	1778/1779	Paired boat	Sprit	Forward	Tack
Mangareva	1826	Log raft	Lateen	Amidships	?
Tonga	1827	Paired boat	Lateen	Amidships	?
New Zealand	1843	Single boat	Sprit?	Forward	Tack
Tonga	1843	Paired boat	Lateen	Amidships	?
Tonga	1843	Single Outrigger	Lateen	Amidships	?
Society Is.	1843	Single Outrigger	Sprit	Amidships	?

Micronesia

		Craft	Sail	Mast	Tack/Shunt
Ladrones	1521	Single Outrigger	Lateen	Amidships	Shunt
Ladrones	1686	Single Outrigger	Lateen	Amidships	Shunt
Carolines	1827	Single Outrigger	Lateen	Amidships	?†
Carolines	1830	Single Outrigger	Lateen	Amidships	Shunt
Carolines	1843	Single Outrigger	Lateen	Amidships	Shunt†
Marianas	1843	Single Outrigger	Lateen	Amidships	?

Melanesia

		Craft	Sail	Mast	Tack/Shunt
Admiralty Is.	1792	Single Outrigger	‡	?	?†
New Guinea	1827	Double Outrigger	‡	?	?
Fiji	1827	Single Outrigger	Lateen	Amidships	?
Santa Cruz	1827	Single Outrigger	Lateen	Amidships	?†
Fiji	1829	Paired boat	Lateen	Amidships	Shunt
Santa Cruz	1843	Single Outrigger	Lateen?	Amidships	?†
New Ireland	1843	Single Outrigger	Lateen	Amidships	?†

† Vessel had balance board.
‡ Rectangular, canted with boom.

America

America was populated across the Bering Strait, possibly via a land bridge at a time of low sea level (back endpaper). Present evidence indicates that from c 30 000 BC (Clark, 1977, 353) Man spread southwards to reach Chile by the mid-10th millennium BC and the southern tip of South America by the mid-9th millennium. Although much of the territory between the Seward Peninsular in Alaska and Tierra del Fuego in the south could have been occupied on foot, this movement would have been greatly facilitated by water transport. The Vikings made a brief appearance on the north-east coast in the 11th century AD and other early contacts have been claimed for the Phoenicians, the Egyptians, the Irish (Morison, 1971, 3–31) and from the Canary Islands (Heyerdahl, 1978, 96–123). It is generally held, however, that (apart from local movements across the Bering Strait) there was no significant contact with other cultures until the European voyages of exploration in the late 15th and early 16th centuries AD.

There is some evidence about the water transport in use before the 16th century, but most information comes from European accounts written at first contact or soon afterwards. The societies the Europeans encountered were at varying stages of technological development, but all were theoretically capable of building the complete array of water transport, and with the exception of the specialised bark bundle rafts and reed boats, all were found in use somewhere in the two continents.

Non-planked craft

Reed rafts　Pottery models from pre-Inca Peru of the early centuries AD are thought to represent reed craft (Clark, 1977, 444; Edwards, 1965, 1). Support for this interpretation comes from excavations by Spahni near the mouth of the River Loa in northern Chile, where a small reed boat model dated c BC/AD has been found (Johnstone, 1980, 14, fig.2.9).

Reed rafts were first sighted by Europeans during Pizarro's voyage of 1531 off the Peruvian coast (Edwards, 1965, 1). Subsequently Acosta found them in use off Callao, Peru, in 1590 and described how they were dismantled and drained after use. De la Vega, who saw them being used for river ferries and for sea fishing, stated that they were made of two reed bundles tapering from the stern to a raised and pointed bow. In 1653 Cobo described similar ones propelled by pole or paddle and also some which were double-ended; sometimes two large ones were joined together to make a raft capable of carrying horses and cattle.

Reed bundle craft were also in use off the coast of northern Chile in 1553, and in the inland waters of 17th century Argentina and 18th century Bolivia (Edwards, 1965, 8–13). In this century they have been used inland in Ecuador, Peru and Brazil and in the coastal waters of Peru (Plate 1), Chile and Brazil. Edwards (1965, 4, 11, 102) who surveyed the craft still in use, believes that the general design and construction has not changed from early post-

Conquest times, except for the introduction of manufactured twine instead of hand-twisted cord to bind the bundles. There is insufficient evidence at present to determine whether or not sail was used on these craft before the Conquest, although the Lake Titicaca rafts now have a rectangular reed-matting sail on a bipod mast.

Further north, early Spanish chroniclers recorded reed rafts on Mexican inland waters and some were in use there in recent times (Thompson, 1949, 74). They were also noted in the early 19th century along the Pacific coast of North America from Mexico to British Columbia, and inland in the Great Basin of western USA and on the rivers and lakes of California (Hornell, 1970, 44–6). Earlier use in these regions, whilst probable, cannot yet be demonstrated.

Thus, apart from their recent use in eastern Brazil, the distribution is, and has been, principally west coast. European observers from the 16th to the 20th centuries agree that these rafts could be operated through surf on open coasts in conditions which would have been hazardous to planked boats.

Buoyed rafts   Light cane platforms on top of two inflated sealskin floats were used by fishermen off the surf-beaten shores of Peru and Chile at first European contact. They were noted by da León in 1553, Acosta in 1590 (Edwards, 1965, 17) and Cavendish in 1587 (Hornell, 1970, 32), and Paris (1843) saw one in Valparaiso in 1834 (Plate 50). In the early 18th century Frezier described how the skins were joined by inserting toggles in holes pierced through the overlap, and then lashed with seal intestines: the floats were inflated through a quille. In the early 20th century Latcham noted the floats were waterproofed with a mixture of clay, grease and oil (Hornell, 1970, 33). At first contact they were propelled by paddle but by the 18th century they had a sail (Edwards, 1965, 18).

Gourds (*calabazas* = dried fruit) netted together were given a light wooden platform and used as ferries in northern Peru where they were seen and used by members of Pizarro's expedition in the 1530s (Edwards, 1965, 59–60), being propelled by swimmers. Hornell (1970, 38–9) has noted that similar rafts were recently used in Mexico and Central America. Thompson (1949, 73) has suggested that the rafts depicted on a gold disc from the early site of Chichen Itza were buoyed by gourds, thus taking their use back 1000 years or so, although Edwards (1965, 92) has pointed out this must have been outside the Chichen Itza region, which has no rivers or lakes on which such a craft could have been used.

Log rafts   Log rafts, with and without sail, are well documented in South American first contact reports and in the early chronicles (Edwards, 1965, 61). Simple rafts made of logs lashed or pinned together and propelled by paddle and pole were used extensively on the rivers of Colombia, Ecuador, Peru,

Plate 50   Drawing by Admiral Paris of a 19th century sealskin raft in Valparaiso, Chile.

Chile, Mexico and Panama as ferries and for fishing. Some were shaped, that is the central log was longer than the others, and some tapered in breadth towards the bow. Raised platforms were built on some rafts for goods or important passengers, and occasionally they had straw huts.

Large seagoing rafts with two masts, cotton sails and hemp rigging were seen by men of Pizarro's 1531 voyage to Peru, and Edwards (1965, 67–9) has demonstrated that their sails were probably triangular rather than square as previous commentators had believed. On the other hand, Heyerdahl (1978, 199) has drawn attention to a model raft with a square reed sail excavated from a grave at Arica, Chile and dated to the early centuries AD. If it was not already in use, the square sail on a bipod mast was probably adopted after the conquest as it appears to be shown on Benzoni's drawing of 1572.

Seagoing rafts could carry large loads on long voyages. The first seen by the Spaniards was said to

Plate 51 Early 17th century drawing by Spilbergen of a sailing log raft with *guares* in Paita harbour, Peru. From de Bry, 1619, plate XII.

have space sufficient for 30 large casks (30 *toneles*), and Dampier recorded in the late-17th century that rafts sailed from Lima to Panama (over 1500 miles) carrying 60–70 *tuns* of goods (Edwards, 1965, 72, 105). Spilbergen's 1619 drawing (Plate 51) of a raft with triangular sails in Paita harbour, Peru shows the use of adjustable boards projecting down between the logs to alter course and vary the sailing balance as well as to reduce leeway. This technique was first documented by the Spanish navigator Juan in the 1730s (Edwards, 1965, 73–4): up to six of these *guares* could be in use, variable in position and in depth of immersion; if one near the bow was immersed more deeply the raft would luff-up (turn towards the wind); raising one near the stern would have a similar effect. Objects of hardwood which are probably *guares* have been excavated from coastal grave sites in Peru. They have an aerofoil cross-section and a hand grip at one end (Heyerdahl, 1978, 102, 197, 205–10); and the earliest has been dated to *c* 300BC. Admiral Paris (1843) shows *guares* on his drawing of a sailing raft from Guayaquil, Ecuador (Johnstone, 1980, 224, fig.16.5) and they have been used in the present century (Edwards, 1965, plate 20).

Log rafts were seen in use on the eastern side of South America by the early Portuguese, but the use of sail was not mentioned (Edwards, 1965, 97). However, the *jangada* a small raft with a triangular sail and *guares* is used today by fishermen off the Brazilian coast. Its details appear to have been documented only from the early 19th century and pre-Conquest use cannot be demonstrated.

Further north, de Ulloa saw log rafts off the coast of Lower California in 1540 (Best, 1925, 142); and Johnstone (1980, 232–3) has drawn attention to two pre-Columbian gold model rafts from Colombia. Waugh (1919, 32) has noted the recent use of rafts by Canadian Indians, and Suder (1930, 85) noted their use in the Caribbean earlier this century.

Bark boats   North American bark boats (Plate 52) were first mentioned by Cartier in 1535 and in 1603 both Champlain and Weymouth commented on the speed and the fine workmanship of canoes seen near Quebec and on the coast of Maine (Adney and Chapelle, 1964, 7). Subsequently bark canoes of varied form were found in use in an area extending almost across the Continent from *c* 60°N to 45°N in the west and 35°N in the east (Hornell, 1970, 186; Waugh, 1919, 24, 29). In the south-east of this area elm, buttonwood and basswood bark were used; on the west coast pine and spruce. But the main area of use coincided with the distribution of the canoe birch (*Betula papyrifera*) which had the most suitable bark for canoe building (Waugh, 1919, 23).

Baron de la Hontan wrote in 1684 the earliest surviving account of how these boats were built (Adney and Chapelle, 1964, 8–10). By this date there had been over a century of French influence in this area of eastern Canada and the effect of this on indigenous canoe-building is problematic. Certainly the French took to the canoe as the most suitable boat for the vast areas of inland waterways, and had a canoe-building factory near Montreal by the middle of the 18th century (Adney and Chapelle, 1964, 13). Adney and Chapelle (1964, 8–10) believe that the longest birch canoes encountered by Europeans in the early years were only *c* 30 ft in length,

and they consider that the large 'war canoes' of the later period were stimulated, if not actually first built, by the French.

The largest boats de la Hontan noted were about 33 ft × 5 ft × 2 ft, made from birch bark *c* $\frac{1}{8}$ in thick with an inner lining of cedar sheeting, an inserted framework of light cedar stringers, many ribs and eight or nine cross members. They were propelled by pole or paddle, the crew kneeling, sitting or standing as appropriate. Sails of blanket, bark, skin or even a bush are known to have been used on occasions by north American Indians (Waugh, 1919, 30) in recent times, but Adney and Chapelle (1964, 10) think aboriginal use is unlikely.

Adney recorded the methods used to build bark canoes in the late 19th and early 20th centuries in several regions of North America (Adney and Chapelle, 1964, 4), and found two principal techniques. In the first, a bark sheet—extended in length and breadth when necessary by other pieces sewn to it with flexible black spruce roots (Waugh, 1919, 26)—was shaped on the ground around the assembled top stringers. Appropriate gores were cut and the bark skin fashioned to give the required sheerline. The stringers were then lifted to sheer level and the top edge of the bark sewn to them. The formation of the stringers, which were a pattern for the plan of the boat, and the shaping of the bark skin may formerly

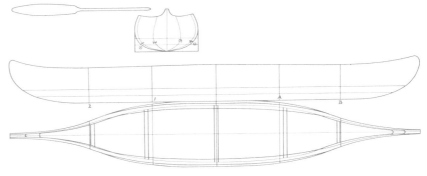

Plate 52   Lines of a New England birchbark canoe brought to Chatham in 1749. Length 18 ft, breadth 2 ft 9½ in, depth 1 ft 6 in. After draught in National Maritime Museum.

have been done by eye, but in the early 20th century sticks ('boat-ells') were marked with the main measurements of the stringer plan and certain heights of the sheerline (Adney and Chapelle, 1964, 37). Ribs were then forced into position to tension the bark skin, which was elastic when green, and a few light cross timbers were fitted at sheer level. The finished canoe was waterproofed with a paying of spruce gum.

When flared sides were required a building 'frame', shorter and less broad than the sheer plan, determined the form of the bottom of the boat. Generally this 'frame' was dismantled and removed from the boat so that it could be used as a pattern for others, although in some Alaskan boats it became part of the internal structure (Adney and Chapelle, 1964, 37, 54–5).

The North American birch bark therefore seems to have been built by a form of shell technique, but in recent times measurement aids have been used to obtain the required shape, rather than 'by eye'.

The differences of form seen in boats of different tribes are probably due to differences of use and operating environment (Adney and Chapelle, 1964, 12, 27). For example, the pointed extension of the lower ends of the Salish bark boats of southern British Columbia are said to be specially adapted to the fast-flowing rivers of the western seaboard (Waugh, 1919, 24). Beothuk canoes of Newfoundland with their sharp V-shaped bottom are said to have been used for open sea voyages to offshore islands and from Newfoundland to Labrador (Adney and Chapelle, 1964, 98); otherwise bark canoes were inland craft.

In South America bark boats were noticed by the first Spaniards to visit southern Chile in 1553 (Edwards, 1965, 21). The Alacalufs and the Yahgans of the far south sewed sheets of bark together with baleen, with laths holding a caulking of straw or

reed under the stitches (Plate 6). In the mid-18th century whilst surveying the Straits of Magellan, Cordoba and others saw boats c 25 ft × 4 ft × 2–3 ft made from three bark sheets. After these sheets had been stitched together to form the hull, ribs, stringers, a bark lining and occasional light cross timbers were inserted and lashed with dried reeds. Edwards (1965, 23) considers that, apart from Cordoba's report of a sealskin sail, unknown before the late 17th century, this account is probably very similar to the aboriginal design.

In the early 20th century simple, single-piece bark canoes were used in Guiana and on the Amazon in Brazil. A slight sheer kept the open ends clear of the water, and cross members gave the bark shell some transverse support (Hornell, 1970, 183–6; Brindley, 1924).

Skin boats　A simple form of skin boat, the *pelota*, is known to have been used in Colombia, Venezuela, Uruguay, Bolivia and Chile from at least the 18th century. Often it had no inserted framework, reliance being placed on the stiffness of an untanned, dried ox-skin to maintain the roughly quadrangular shape (Hornell, 1970, 150). When a light internal framework was added it was lashed to the skin by thongs. Such boats are not mentioned in the early Spanish chronicles and the absence of cattle and horses from pre-Columbian South America may indicate that this is not an aboriginal form of water transport. Hornell (1970, 153–4) has argued, however, that in earlier times, skins of the native guanaco may have been sewn together to produce a covering of sufficient size for a boat. Thompson (1949, 74) mentions a tradition in eastern Mexico of the former use of plaited withies waterproofed with clay – possibly a form of skin boat, but its date is unclear.

The 'bull boat' (Plate 7) of the Plains Indians of North America had a simple framework of willow rods and withies, lashed together with rawhide, which was covered by one or two buffalo hides (Hornell, 1970, 148–9). Other skin boats used by North American Indians were built in a bark canoe sequence, that is using the top stringers as a mould, and then forcing ribs into the skin hull (Adney and Chapelle, 1964, 219–20).

The best known skin boats of America are the Eskimo *umiak* and *kayak* (Plate 53) seen to be in use at first European contact (Hornell, 1970, 155) around the coast of Alaska, the northern coast and islands of Canada, and Labrador and Greenland. These are similar to the *baidara* and the *baidarka* of the Bering Strait and eastern Siberia (see p.27). These two types exemplify the evolution of craft well adapted to a specific environment and function. The building method described by Billings in 1802 (see p.27) is very similar to that used this century for Russian and Canadian boats (Hornell, 1970, 156–9). Twentieth century details not mentioned by Billings are the fastening of stem and sternposts to the keelson when building the *umiak* framework and the extension of the top stringers beyond the ends to form handles.

Details of the early 18th century *kayaks* are known from one recovered off the Scottish coast and now in Marischal College, Aberdeen. It is similar in shape to recent ones, and has a light framework of wood and willow branches covered by skin except for the round opening for the crew (Hornell, 1970, 164).

Logboats   A logboat of white oak from Lake Eyrie has been dated by radiocarbon to *c* 1600 bc (*Art & Archaeology Technical Abstracts*, 15.2, 1978, 75), and four of pine from Florida have dates in the 4th to 14th centuries AD (UM-1449, 1450, 1451, 1625).

Logboats were noticed at first European contact but were seldom recorded in sufficient detail to indicate whether they were simple logboats or had been extended by the addition of washstrakes, or whether their stability had been increased by expansion or by the use of stabilisers. In 1492 Columbus encountered West Indian logboats that could carry 70 or 80 men, and one he saw on his second voyage measured 96 ft × 8 ft (Johnstone, 1980, 234). Ecuadorian river logboats with sail were seen during Pizarro's 1531 voyage, but details were not recorded (Edwards, 1965, 35).

Plate 53   Measured drawing of an 18th century *kayak* from north eastern Canada. Length 21 ft 6 in, breadth 2 ft 2½ in. After original drawing in National Maritime Museum.

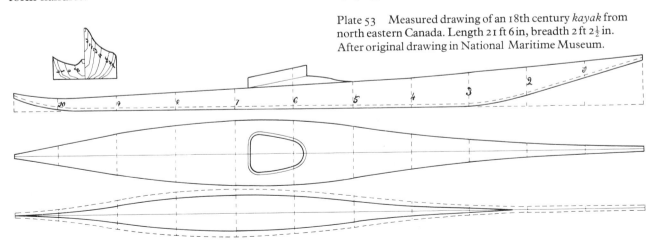

Thompson (1949, 71–2) has noted several early reports of logboats with sail in the West Indies, Mexico, Panama and Honduras. Logboats were also reported from the western coast of Colombia, Florida and Virginia in the 16th century (Edwards, 1965, 36–7; Durham, 1955, 34; Johnstone, 1980, 235–5; Quinn, 1973, 6; Thompson, 1949, 69). The best documented logboats seem to be those of British Columbia (variants are known as *salish, chinook, haida, nootka*). These were noted by Cook and drawn by Weber in 1778 (Rienits, 1968, 140), and noted by Meares in 1788–9 and Vancouver in 1792. Recent descriptions by Waugh (1919), Longstaff (1930) and Durham (1955) indicate that there were only minor changes between the 18th and 20th centuries.

In the 19th century logboats were seen by Paris (1843) in Valparaiso, Chile and Calloa, Peru. They were recently used by the Iroquois, from south of Lake Ontario, the Yakutat Indians of S.W. Alaska and in Guiana, the Upper Amazon and Argentinian Patagonia, Michigan, Wisconsin, on the lower Mississippi, Arkansas, Louisiana and generally in eastern USA. It might seem therefore that logboats were used in parts of prehistoric America other than in those regions where they were noted by early Europeans. However, it is known that the Spaniards introduced logboats to Peru and Chile (Edwards, 1965, 108) and there may be other undocumented post-European introductions giving rise to the 19th and 20th century distribution.

There are several early accounts of how logboats were built, some more detailed than others (Edwards, 1965, 3, 7, 104; Quinn, 1973, 6; Waugh, 1919, 32): generally they are variations of a standard method (McGrail, 1978, 28–36). There are no early accounts of expansion but the practice is known from recent times in Guiana, Brazil, Tierra del Fuego, British Columbia, and south-west Alaska (McGrail, 1978, 38–9).

Boats of sewn planks

At the time of first European contact boats with sewn planks were in use in two widely separated places on the western seaboard of America, off southern Chile and southern California. In Chile, between the Gulf of Coronados (north of the island of Chiloe) and the Gulf of Penas (south of the Chonos archipelago), a three-plank, sewn *dalca* was seen by members of de Ulloa's 1553 expedition and used by a Spanish expedition of 1558 (Edwards, 1965, 25). In 1560 de Góngora Marmolejo recorded that these boats were some 30–40 ft × 3 ft and that the planking was fastened by thin cords with the seams made watertight by crushed bark held in position by longitudinal split canes. Quoting early 17th century accounts, Lothrop (1932, 244–5) states that wedges were used to split larch (*Fitzroya patagonica*), cypress (*Libocedrus tetragona*) or beech (*Nothofagus betuloides*) logs into planks which were then finished with stone and shell tools. The sewing fibre was prepared from bamboo (*Chusquea coleu*), and the material in the seams was inner bark of the maqui (*Aristolelia maqui*), leaves of the *tiaca* (*Caldeluvia paniculata*) or rolls of grass. Later descriptions indicate that their general form was similar to the bark boats used further south, but they were somewhat broader at the ends with the bottom plank curving upwards to form long overhangs obtained by softening the planking with fire and water and bending it against stakes driven into the ground (Edwards, 1965, 103; Lothrop, 1932, 244, 245, fig.6). The only internal structure appears to have been sticks used as thwarts, floor timbers not being added until the late-18th century. As later Spaniards had to modify them to take oars it may be assumed that previously they were paddled, the crew being nine to eleven men (Lothrop, 1932, 245). In 1675 de Vea transported dismantled *dalcas* across the Isthmus of Ofquí and reassembled them; this probably reflects aboriginal usage (Edwards, 1965, 26).

In the region of the Santa Barbara Channel near Los Angeles in southern California, the Chumash Indians used a sewn plank boat, the *tomolo* (Heizer, 1966). The earliest report is from Cabrillo's expedition of 1542, and from this and subsequent accounts up to that of Vancouver in 1793, Heizer has deduced the form and construction of these boats. It should be noted however that Kroeber (1925, 812) considered that the *tomolo* might be a logboat with added washstrakes rather than a true planked boat. Heizer (1966, 28–9) concluded that the planking was split from driftwood logs of cedar, pine and redwood using whalebone wedges. The bottom plank was c 12–14ft × 8–10in × $1\frac{1}{2}$ in, whilst the remainder were much smaller, and they were fastened together and to the stem and stern posts by fibre or sinew cords with a caulking of bitumen: subsequently the entire hull was payed with bitumen. The only internal structure was a single thwart amidships. The boats were generally double-ended with sheer at the ends and they were 3 to 4ft broad with lengths from 12 to 26ft. *Tomolo* were propelled by double-bladed paddles and used in the relatively sheltered waters protected by the islands of Santa Barbara, Santa Rosa and San Miguel. This topography and the local source of bitumen may not only have stimulated the evolution of the *tomolo* but also limited its distribution.

The documentation of the *tomolo* is unsatisfactory, in particular, some of the features attributed to it may have been acquired from Europeans. Nevertheless, the use of sewn planks in the Santa Barbara region at first European contact seems to be authentic, but possibly for extended logboats rather than fully planked boats.

Glossary

ad = date in radiocarbon years
AD = date in calendar years
Approximate conversion:
AD = ad + (20 to 70) years in 1st Millennium ad.

Aspect ratio ratio of (height)^2 of sail to area.

bc = date in radiocarbon years
BC = date in calendar years
Approximate conversion:
BC = bc + (100 to 300) years in 1st Millennium bc.
BC = bc + (200 to 500) years in 2nd Millennium bc.

Braces lines to trim yard to wind.

Caulk to insert material between two members and thus make the junction watertight. Whether this is done before or after the planking is assembled may be an important diagnostic trait.

Ceiling lining of planking over *floor timbers*.

Cleat a projection to which other fittings may be fastened.

Clinker a form of boatbuilding in which the *strakes* are placed so that they partly overlap one another – usually upper strake outboard of lower strake.

Crook a curved piece of wood which has grown into a shape useful for boatbuilding.

Double-ended a boat which is (nearly) symmetrical about the midships transverse plane.

Draft (draught) vertical distance from the lowest point of the hull to the waterline.

Draw-tongued joint a method of fastening *flush-laid* planking in which free tenons are fitted into mortices cut in the meeting edges of adjacent planks; after the planking is assembled the tenons are generally pierced by two treenails, one through each plank. Sometimes known as 'mortice and tenon'.

Floor timber a transverse member—often a *crook*—extending from turn of bilge to turn of bilge (see *frame*)

Flush-laid planking in which adjoining *strakes* are butted and do not overlap.

Frame a transverse member made up of more than one piece of timber, usually extending from *sheer* to *sheer* and set against the planking.

Freeboard vertical distance from the *sheerline* amidships to the waterline.

Halyard line to hoist and lower sails.

Heel end of *keel* and lower part of stem or sternpost.

Hood-end end of *strake* fastened to stem or sternpost.

Joggled notched to fit close against another *timber*.

Keel central longitudinal timber in a planked boat's bottom, of deep cross section.

Keel-plank central bottom plank thicker than others. With bottom planks all of same thickness boat is *keel-less*.

Knee a naturally grown *crook* used as a bracket between two members set at about right-angles to each other.

L/B; L/D L/B = length/breadth ratio; L/D = length/depth ratio.

Logboat, expanded a basic logboat enlarged by forcing the sides apart.

Logboat, extended a basic or *expanded* logboat with the height of the sides increased by the addition of a *washstrake(s)*. As more washstrakes are added it becomes indistinguishable from a planked boat.

Mast-step fitting to locate bottom end of mast.

Moulds transverse wooden patterns giving shape of vessel.

Outrigger framework of boom(s) and float(s) projecting from the side(s) of a boat.

Rabbet groove worked in a *timber* to accept another.

Rib simple form of *frame*.

Rocker fore-and-aft curvature of *keel* or bottom of vessel.

Scarf a tapered or wedge shaped joint between pieces of similar section at the join.

Seam juncture of two members required to be watertight.

Sheer (line) the curve of the upper edge of the hull.

Sheets lines to trim sail to wind.

Shell sequence of construction a method of boatbuilding in which the watertight shell (stems, keel and planking in a planked boat; bark skin in a bark boat) is built or partly built before the floor timbers or other internal structure are fitted (see *Skeleton*).

Shrouds ropes leading from the mast head to the sides of the boat to support the mast athwartships.

Skeleton sequence of construction a method of boatbuilding in which a framework giving the essential form of the boat is erected before the waterproof *shell* (planking in a planked boat; skin in a skin boat) is added (see *Shell*).

Stabilisers external *timbers* fastened along waterline.

Stays ropes leading from the masthead forward and aft, to support the mast.

Strake a single plank or combination of planks which stretches from one end of the boat to the other.

Strake, transition the *strake* at the transition between bottom and sides of a boat—especially when there is a marked change in the boat's transverse section.

Stringer a longitudinal strength member along the inside of the planking.

Tack lower forward corner of sail.

Thickness gauges holes bored to pre-set depths into a log which is to be hollowed, to indicate the required thickness of bottom (and sides).

Thole a wooden or bone projection at *sheer* level providing a pivot for an oar.

Thwart a transverse member used as a seat.

Timbers generally: pieces of wood used in boat or shipbuilding.

Transom athwartship bulkhead; in this text it is normally applied to a fitted bulkhead at the stern or the bow. Bulkheads are a form of transom.

Treenail wooden peg or through-fastening used to join two members. It may be secured at each or either end by the insertion of a wedge.

Wale a *strake* thicker than the rest.

Washstrake an additional *strake* normally fitted to keep out spray and water; in this text it is applied to any *strake* fitted to a basic or *expanded* logboat.

References

Adney,E.T., and Chapelle,H.I., 1964, *Bark Canoes and Skin Boats of North America*, Washington.

Åkerlund,H., 1963, *Nydamskeppen*, Göteborg.

Ammerman,A.J., 1979, 'A study of obsidian exchange networks in Colabria', *World Archaeology*, 11, 95-110.

Anderson,A.O., and M.O., 1961 (ed), *Adomnan's Life of St. Columba*.

Anderson,B.W., 1978, *Living World of the Old Testament*, 3rd edition.

Arnold,B., 1978, 'Gallo-Roman Boat finds in Switzerland' in Taylor,J.du P., and Cleere,H., (ed) *Roman Shipping and Trade*, 31-5, CBA Research Report 24.

Audemard,L., 1957, *Les Jonques Chinoises*, Volume 1, Rotterdam.

Bass,G., 1972, *History of Seafaring*.

Bass,G.F., 1978, 'Glass Treasure from the Aegean', *National Geographic Magazine*, 153, 768-92.

Bellwood,P., 1978, *The Polynesians*.

Best,E., 1925, *Maori Canoe*, Wellington. (Dominion Museum Bulletin 7.)

Birdsell,J.H., 1977, 'Recalibration of a paradigm for the first peopling of Greater Australia' in Allen,J., *et al.*, (ed) *Sunda and Sahul*, 113-68.

Bowen,R.le B., 1952, 'Primitive watercraft of Arabia', *American Neptune*, 12, 186-221.

Bowen, R.le B., 1956, 'Boats of the Indus civilisation', *Mariner's Mirror*, 42, 279-90.

Bradley,R., 1978, *Prehistoric settlement of Britain*.

Brindley,H.H., 1919-20, 'Notes on the boats of Siberia', *Mariner's Mirror*, 5, 66-72, 101-17, 130-42, 184-7; 6, 15-18, 187.

Brindley,H.H., 1931, 'Sailing balsa of L. Titicaca and other reed bundle craft', *Mariner's Mirror*, 17, 7-19.

Brindley,M.D., 1924, 'Canoes of British Guiana', *Mariner's Mirror*, 10, 124-32.

Brøgger,A.W., and Shetelig,H., 1971, *Viking Ships*.

Bruce-Mitford,R., 1975, *Sutton Hoo ship burial*, vol.1.

Brusic,Z., 1968, 'Istrazibanje anticke luke Kod Nina', *Diadora*, 4, 203-9.

Camps,G., 1976, 'La navigation' in Guitaine,J., (ed) *La La Préhistoire Française*, II, 192-201.

Casson,L., 1963, 'Sewn Boats', *Classical Review*, 13, 257-9.

Casson,L., 1971, *Ships and Seamanship in the Ancient World*, Princeton.

Casson,L., 1980, 'Two-masted Greek ships', *International Journal of Nautical Archaeology*, 9, 68-9.

Christensen,A.E., 1972A, 'Scandinavian ships from earliest times to the Vikings', in Bass,G.F. (ed), 1972.

Christensen,A.E., 1972B, 'Boatbuilding tools and the process of learning' in Hasslöf,O., *et al.*, (ed) *Ships and Shipyards, Sailors and Fishermen*, 235-59, Copenhagen.

Christensen,A.E., 1979, 'Viking Age Rigging' in McGrail, 1979A, 183-94.

Christie,A., 1957, 'An obscure passage from the Periplus', *Bulletin of the London School of African Studies*, 19, 345-53.

Clark,G., 1952, *Prehistoric Europe: the economic basis*.

Clark,G., 1977, *World Prehistory*, 3rd edition, Cambridge.

Clark,G., and Piggott,S., 1976, *Prehistoric Societies*.

Coles,J.M., and Harding,A.F., 1979, *Bronze Age in Europe*.

Crumlin-Pedersen,O., 1965, 'Cog-kogge-kaag', *Handels og Sjøfartsmuseum pa Kronberg Arbog*, 81-144.

Crumlin-Pedersen,O., 1969, *Das Haithabuschiff*, Neumünster.

Crumlin-Pedersen,O., 1972A, 'Vikings and the Hanseatic merchants' in Bass, 1972, 181-204.

Crumlin-Pedersen,O., 1972B, 'Skin or Wood' in Hasslöf,O., *et al.*, (ed) *Ships and Shipyards, Sailors and Fishermen*, Copenhagen.

Crumlin-Pedersen,O., 1978, 'Ships of the Vikings' in Andersson,T., and Sandred,K.I., (ed) *The Vikings*, 32-41, Uppsala.

Crumlin-Pedersen,O., 1979, 'Danish Cog finds' in McGrail, 1979A, 17-34.

de Boe,G., 1978, 'Roman boats from a small river harbour at Pommeroeul, Belgium' in Taylor,J.du P., and Cleere,H., 1978, *Roman shipping and trade*, 22-30, CBA Research Report 24.

de Bry,T. (1601-1629):
   1602   *Grands Voyages*, part 9, 1st Latin edition.
   1619   *Grands Voyages*, part 11, Latin edition.
   1601   *Petits Voyages*, part 5, Latin edition.
   1629   *Petits Voyages*, part 3, 2nd Latin edition.

de Laguna,F., 1963, 'Yakutat Canoes', *Folk*, 5, 219-29, Copenhagen.

Delaney,J., 1976, 'Fieldwork in south Roscommon' in
Ó Danochair,C., (ed) *Folk and Farm*, 15-29, Dublin.

Denford,G.T., and Farrell,A.W., 1980, 'Caergwrle bowl',
International Journal of Nautical Archaeology, 9, 183-192.

de Weerd,M.D., 1978, 'Ships of the Roman period at
Zwammerdam/Nigrum Pullum, Germania Inferior' in
Taylor,J.du P., and Cleere,H., (ed) *Roman shipping and
trade*, 15-21, CBA Research Report, 24.

de Weerd,M.D., and Haalebos,J.K., 1973, 'Schepen voor
het Opscheppen', *Spiegel Historiael*, 8, 386-97.

Doran,E., 1973, *Nao, Junk and Vaka*, Texas.

Doran,E., 1978, 'Seaworthiness of Sailing Rafts', *Anthropological Journal of Canada*, 16, 17-22.

Doran,J.E., and Hodson,F.R., 1975, *Mathematics and
Computers in Archaeology*, Edinburgh.

Dumont d'Urville,J.S.C., 1834-5, *Voyage pittoresque autour
du monde*, Vol.1, 1834, Vol.2, 1835, Paris.

Durham,G., 1955, 'Canoes from Cedar Logs', *Pacific
Northwest Quarterly*, 46, 33-9.

Edwards,C.R., 1965, *Aboriginal Watercraft on the Pacific
Coast of S. America*, Ibero-Américáná, 47, University of
California.

Ellmers,D., 1969, 'Keltischer Schiffbau', *Jahrbuch des
Römisch-Germanischen Zentralmuseums Mainz*, 16, 73-122.

Ellmers,D., 1972, *Frühmittelalterliche Handelsschiffahrt in
Mittel und Nordeuropa*, Neumünster.

Ellmers,D., 1973, 'Kultbarken, fahren, fischerboote,
vorgeschichtliche einbäume in Niedersachsen', *Die Kunde*,
NS24, 23-62.

Ellmers,D., 1975, 'Antriebstechniken Germanischer schiffe
im I Jahrtausend N. CHR', *Deutsches Schiffahrtsarchiv*,
1, 80-90.

Ellmers,D., 1978, 'Shipping on the Rhine during the
Roman period' in Taylor,J.du P., and Cleere,H., (ed)
Roman Shipping and Trade, 1-14, CBA Research Report
24.

Ellmers,D., 1979, 'Cog of Bremen and related boats' in
McGrail, 1979A, 1-16.

Farrell,A.W., 1979, 'Use of iconographic material in
Medieval Ship Archaeology', in McGrail (ed), 1979A,
227-46.

Farrell,A.W., and Penny,S., 1975, 'Broighter boat: a
re-assessment', *Irish Archaeological Research Forum*, 2.2,
15-26.

Fenwick,V., 1978, *Graveney Boat*, BAR 53, NMM Archaeological Series 3.

Fliedner,S., 1972, *Cog of Bremen*, Bremen.

Folkard,H.C., 1870, *The Sailing Boat*.

Gillmer,T., 1979, 'Capability of the single square sail rig' in
McGrail, 1979A, 167-82.

Gordon,R.K., 1949, *Anglo Saxon Poetry*.

Greenhill,B., 1971, *Boats and Boatmen of Pakistan*, Newton
Abbott.

Greenhill,B., 1976, *Archaeology of the boat*.

Haddon,A.C., and Hornell,J., *Canoes of Oceania*, Honolulu:
(1936) Vol.1   Polynesia, Fiji and Micronesia.
(1937) Vol.2   Melanesia, Queensland and New Guinea.
(1938) Vol.3   Terms, General Survey and Conclusions.

Hale,J.R., 1980, 'Plank-built in the Bronze Age', *Antiquity*,
54, 118-27.

Hallam,B.R., *et al.*, 1976, 'Obsidian in the western Mediterranean', *Proceedings of the Prehistoric Society*, 42, 85-110.

Hawkes,C.F.C., 1975, *Pytheas*, Oxford.

Heizer,R.F., 1966, 'Plank canoes of South and North
America', *Kroeber Anthropological Society Papers*, 35,
22-39.

Heyerdahl,T., 1972, *The Ra Expeditions*.

Heyerdahl,T., 1978, *Early Man and the Ocean*.

Hill,A.H., 1958, 'Some early accounts of the oriental boat',
Mariner's Mirror, 44, 201-17.

Hin,H.C., and Ng,B., 1974, 'Sha Tsui, High Island', *J.
Hong Kong Archaeological Society*, 5, 28-33.

Hodges,H., 1970, *Technology in the Ancient World*.

Hoekstra,T.J., 1975, 'Utrecht', *International Journal of
Nautical Archaeology*, 4, 390-2.

Hornell,J., 1970, *Water Transport: origins and early evolution*, Cambridge, reprinted 1970, Newton Abbott.

Horridge,G.A., 1978, *Design of Planked Boats of the
Moluccas*, NMM Greenwich, Monograph 38.

Horridge,G.A., 1979A, *Lambo or Prahu Bot*, NMM
Greenwich, Monograph 39.

Horridge,G.A., 1979B, *Konjo Boatbuilders and the Bugis
Prahus of S. Sulawesi*, NMM Greenwich, Monograph 40.

Hourani,G.F., 1963, *Arab Seafaring*, Beirut (Khayats
Oriental Reprints No.3).

Hulst,R.S., and L.Th.Lehmann, 1974, 'The Roman Barge
of Druten', *Berichten van de Rijksdienst voor het
Oudheidkundig Bodemonderzoek*, 24, 7-24.

Huntingford,G.W.B., 1980, (ed) *The Periplus of the
Erythraean Sea*, Hakluyt Society, 2° series, N° 151.

Jacobi,R.M., 1976, 'Britain inside and outside Mesolithic
Europe', *Proceedings Prehistoric Society*, 42, 67-84.

Jellema,D., 1955, 'Frisian trade in the Dark Ages', *Speculum*,
30, 15-36.

Joffroy,R., 1978, 'Note sur deux ferrets Mérovingiens de collections du Musée des Antiquités Nationales' in Fleury,M., and Périn,P. (ed) *Problèmes de Chronologie relative et absolue concernant les cimetières mérovingiens d'entre Loire et Rhin*, Paris.

Johnstone,P., 1964, 'Bantry boat', *Antiquity*, 38, 277-84.

Johnstone,P., 1972, 'Bronze Age sea trial', *Antiquity*, 46, 269-74.

Johnstone,P., 1976, 'Shipwrights and Wheelwrights in the Ancient World' in Megaw,J.V.S., (ed) *To illustrate the Monuments*, 49-56.

Johnstone,P., 1980, *Seacraft of Prehistory*.

Johnstone,T.M., and Muir,J., 1962, 'Portuguese influences on shipbuilding in the Persian Gulf', *Mariner's Mirror*, 48, 58-63.

Jones,G., 1964, *Norse Atlantic Saga*.

Keeley,L., 1980, *Experimental determination of stone tool uses*, Chicago.

Kroeber,A.L., 1925, *Handbook of the Indians of California*, Washington.

Lane-Fox,A., 1875, 'On early modes of navigation', *J. Royal Anthropological Institute*, 4, 399-437.

Layard,A.H., 1853, *Discoveries in the ruins of Nineveh and Babylon*.

Lehmann,L.Th., 1978, 'The flat-bottomed Roman boat from Druten, Netherlands', *International Journal of Nautical Archaeology*, 7, 259-67.

Linschoten,J.H.van, 1610, *Histoire de la Navigation*, Amsterdam.

Longstaff,F.V., 1930, 'British Columbian Indian Cedar Dugout Canoes', *Mariner's Mirror*, 16, 259-62.

Lothrop,S.K., 1932, 'Aboriginal navigation off the west coast of S. America', *J. Royal Anthropological Institute*, 62, 229-56.

McCusker,J.J., 1966, 'Wine Prise and Medieval Mercantile Shipping', *Speculum*, 41, 279-96.

McGrail,S., 1975, 'The Brigg "raft" re-excavated', *Lincolnshire History and Archaeology*, 10, 5-13.

McGrail,S., 1977, 'Aspects of Experimental Boat Archaeology' in McGrail,S., (ed) *Sources and Techniques in Boat Archaeology*, BAR S29, NMM Archaeological Series 1.

McGrail,S., 1978, *Logboats of England and Wales*, BAR 51, NMM Archaeological Series 2.

McGrail,S., (ed) 1979A, *Medieval Ships and Harbours in Northern Europe*, BAR S66, NMM Archaeological Series 5.

McGrail,S., 1979B, 'Prehistoric boats, timber, and woodworking technology', *Proceedings Prehistoric Society*, 45, 159-63.

McGrail,S., and Corlett,E., 1977, 'High speed capabilities of ancient boats', *International Journal of Nautical Archaeology*, 6, 352-3.

McGrail,S., and Farrell,A.W., 1979, 'Rowing: aspects of the ethnographic and iconographic evidence', *International Journal of Nautical Archaeology*, 8, 155-66.

McGrail,S., and McKee,E., 1974, *Building and trials of the replica of an ancient boat – Gokstad faering*. NMM Monograph 11.

McGrail,S., and Switsur,R., 1979, 'Logboats of the River Mersey', in McGrail,S. (ed), 1979A, 93-115.

McKusick,M.B., 1960, *Aboriginal Canoes in the West Indies*, Yale University Publication in Anthropology No.63.

Manninen,I., 1927, 'Zur Ethnologie des Einbaumes', *Eurasia Septentrionalis Antiqua*, 1, 4-17.

Marsden,P., 1971, 'Archaeological finds in the City of London 1967-70', *Trans. London & Middlesex Archaeological Society*, 23, 1-14.

Marsden,P., 1976, 'Boat of the Roman period found at Bruges, Belgium in 1899 and related types', *International Journal of Nautical Archaeology*, 5, 23-55.

Marstrander,S., 1963, *Østfolds Jordbruksristninger*, Oslo.

Marstrander,S., 1976, 'Building a hide boat. An archaeological experiment', *International Journal of Nautical Archaeology*, 5, 13-22.

Mookerji,R., 1912, *Indian Shipping*, Bombay.

Morison,S.E., 1971, *European Discoveries of America*, New York.

Morrison,J.S., 1976, 'Classical Traditions', chapter 9 in Greenhill, 1976.

Morrison,J., 1980, *Long Ships and Round Ships*.

Muckelroy,K., Haselgrove,C., and Nash,D., 1978, 'A pre-Roman coin from Canterbury and the ship represented on it', *Proceedings Prehistoric Society*, 44, 439-44.

Müller-Wille,M., 1974, 'Boat-graves in Northern Europe', *Int. J. Nautical Archaeology*, 3, 187-204.

Müllner,A., 1892, 'Ein schiff im Laibacher Moore', *Argo*, 1, 2-8.

Mulvaney,D.J., 1975, *Prehistory of Australia*, Victoria.

Needham,J., 1971, *Sciences and Civilisation in China*, vol.4, part 3, Cambridge.

Nikkilä,E., 1947, 'En Satakundensisk äsping och dess Eurasiska motsvarigheter', *Folk-Liv*, 11, 33-46.

Nishimura,S., 1920, *The Kumano-No-Morota-Bune, or the many-paddled ship of Kumano*, Tokyo.

Nishimura,S., 1925, *Ancient Rafts of Japan*, Tokyo.

Nishimura,S., 1931, *Skinboats (Ancient Ships of Japan, Vols.5,6,7,8)*, Tokyo.

Nishimura,S., 1936, *Hani-bune or Clay boat ; Kako-no-Kawa or Deerskin (Ancient Ships of Japan, Vol.9)*, Tokyo.

Nooteboom,C., 1949, 'Eastern Diremes', *Mariner's Mirror*, 35, 272-5.

Olsen,O., and Crumlin-Pedersen,O., 1967, 'Skuldelev Ships', *Acta Archaeologica*, 38, 73-174.

Paris,F.E., 1843, *Essai sur la Construction Navale des peuples extra-Européens*, Paris.

Philipsen,J.P.W., 1965, 'Utrecht ship', *Mariner's Mirror*, 51, 35-46.

Quinn,D.B., and A.M., 1973, (ed) *Virginian Voyages from Hakluyt*.

Ränk,G., 1933, 'Zwei seltene bootfunde aus Estland', *Sitzungsberichte der Gelchrten Estinschen Gesellschaft*, 304-15.

Rao,S.R., 1965, 'Shipping and maritime trade of the Indus people', *Expedition*, 7, 30-7.

Reinders,R., 1979, 'Medieval Ships: recent finds in the Netherlands', in McGrail, 1979A, 35-44.

Rienits,R. and T., 1968, *Voyages of Captain Cook*.

Riley,W.E., 1912, *Ship of the Roman Period discovered on the New County Hall site* (2nd edition), London County Council.

Robertson,J., 1925, *Laws of the Kings of England from Edmund to Henry I*, Cambridge.

Robinson,C.H., 1921, *Anskar, Apostle of the North*.

Rosenberg,G., 1937, *Hjortspring fundet*, Copenhagen.

Roth,H.L., 1899, *Aborigines of Tasmania*, 2nd edition, Halifax.

Rudolph,W., 1974, *Boats, Rafts, Ships*.

Sauer,M., 1802, *Account of an Expedition to the Northern Parts of Russia by Commodore Joseph Billings*.

Schovsbo,P.O., 1980, 'Mast and sail in Scandinavia in the Bronze Age', *Mariner's Mirror*, 66, 15-16.

Severin,T., 1978, *Brendan Voyage*.

Sheppard,T., 1926, 'Roman remains in north Lincolnshire', *East Riding Antiquarian Society Transactions*, 25, 170-4.

Shetelig,H., 1903, 'Fragments of an old boat from Halsnø', *Årbok Bergen*, 7, 8-21.

Shutler,R., and Shutler,M.E., 1975, *Oceanic Prehistory*, California.

Sieveking,G.de G., 1954, 'Recent Archaeological discoveries in Malaya (1952-3)', *J. Malayan branch of Royal Asiatic Society*, 27, 224-33.

Sieveking,G.de G., 1956, 'Recent archaeological discoveries in Malaya (1955)', *J. Malayan Branch Royal Asiatic Society*, 29, 200-11.

Stenton,F.M., 1967, *Anglo Saxon England*, 2nd edition, Oxford.

Stevenson,W.H., 1959, (ed) *Asser's Life of King Alfred*.

Suder,H., 1930, *Vom Einbaum und Floss zum Schiff*, Berlin.

Taylor,E.G.R., 1971, *Haven-finding art*.

Tchernia,A., *et al.*, 1978, 'L'épave romaine de la Madrague de Giens (var)', *Gallia*, 34th supplement, Paris.

Thesiger,W., 1978, *Marsh Arabs*.

Thompson,J.E.S., 1949, 'Canoes and navigation of the Maya and their neighbours', *J. Royal Anthropological Institute*, 79, 69-78.

Troels-Smith,J., 1946, 'Stammebaade fra Aamonsen', *Nationalmuseets Arbejdsmark*, 15-23, København.

van Doorninck,F.H., 1975, '4th century wreck at Yassi Ada', *International Journal of Nautical Archaeology*, 5, 115-131.

Villain-Gandossi,C., 1979, 'Medieval Ships as shown by Illuminations in French Manuscripts' in McGrail, 1979A, 195-225.

Vinnicombe,P., 1976, *People of the Eland*, Pietermaritzburg.

Waugh,F.W., 1919, 'Canadian Aboriginal Canoes', *Canadian Field Naturalist*, 33, 23-33.

Willetts,W., 1964, 'Maritime Adventures of Grand Eunuch Ho', *J. of S.E. Asian History*, 5, 25-42.

Wilson,D.M., 1966, 'Medieval boat from Kentmere, Westmorland', *Medieval Archaeology*, 10, 81-8.

Worcester,G.R.G., 1956A, 'Origin and observance of the Dragon boat Festival in China', *Mariner's Mirror*, 42, 127-37.

Worcester,G.R.G., 1956B, 'Four small craft of Taiwan', *Mariner's Mirror*, 42, 302-12.

Worcester,G.R.G., 1966, *Sail and Sweep in China*.

Worthington,E.B., 1933, 'Primitive Craft of the Central African Lakes', *Mariner's Mirror*, 19, 146-63.

Wright,E.V., 1976, *The North Ferriby Boats*, NMM Monograph 23.

Index

Types of water transport by name

Sites with a boat or raft or representation

THE SHIP

The complete list of titles in this major series of ten books on the development of the ship is as follows:

1. *Rafts, Boats and Ships From Prehistoric Times to the Medieval Era* Sean McGrail
2. *Long Ships and Round Ships Warfare and Trade in the Mediterranean 3000 BC–500 AD* John Morrison
3. *Tiller and Whipstaff The Development of the Sailing Ship : 1400–1700* Alan McGowan
4. *The Century before Steam The Development of the Sailing Ship : 1700–1820* Alan McGowan
5. *Steam Tramps and Cargo Liners : 1850–1950* Robin Craig
6. *Channel Packets and Ocean Liners : 1850–1970* John M. Maber
7. *The Life and Death of the Merchant Sailing Ship : 1815–1965* Basil Greenhill
8. *Steam, Steel and Torpedoes The Warship in the 19th Century* David Lyon
9. *Dreadnought to Nuclear Submarine* Antony Preston
10. *The Revolution in Merchant Shipping : 1950–1980* Ewan Corlett

All titles in *The Ship* series are available from:
HER MAJESTY'S STATIONERY OFFICE

Government Bookshops

49 High Holborn, London WC1V 6HB
13a Castle Street, Edinburgh EH2 3AR
41 The Hayes, Cardiff CF1 1JW
Brazennose Street, Manchester M60 8AS
Southey House, Wine Street, Bristol BS1 2BQ
258 Broad Street, Birmingham B1 2HE
80 Chichester Street, Belfast BT1 4JY

Government publications are also available through booksellers

The full range of Museum publications is displayed and sold at
National Maritime Museum
Greenwich

HMSO BOOKS

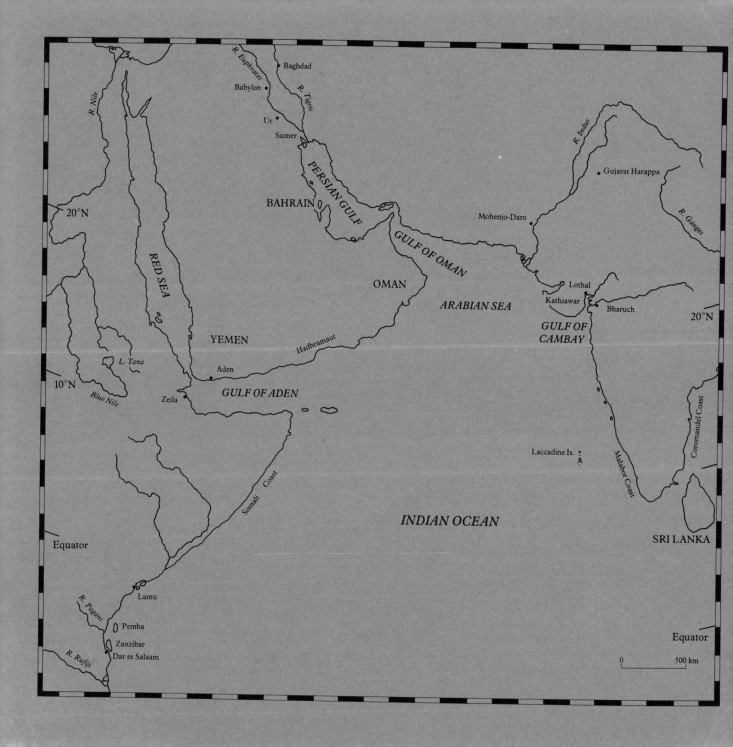